T0323358

THE RULES

Eric Zimmerman

Princeton Architectural Press
New York

WE BREAK

CONTENTS

PLAY

SYSTEMS

A few ways to think about
Systems

Exercises
when you have a couple of hours
to tinker with a system

System Dynamics

Balancing Systems

Narrative Systems

DESIGN

PLAY WITH

THIS
BOOK

Don't read this book. Play with it.
This is not a book of information to learn or facts to absorb. It is a handbook for action. A guide for curating playful situations. A cookbook of recipes for new ways of thinking.

The Rules We Break is based on the principle of *learning by doing*. If you create experiences, manage organizations, collaborate with people, or in any way take part in the production of culture, you are designing. In my experience, design is about doing and living and being. It is less about knowledge and data and more about experimentation and practice. This book is a design manual filled with *things to do*.

I call these things to do "exercises." Just like physical exercises, they are ways of using your body and mind, to train them and make them stronger and more flexible. Each exercise challenges you to interact with other people, solve problems, and think about how things are put together. Some of them are full-body physical games. Others take place on a tabletop. Most of the exercises require limited materials and setup. And all of them can be done without computers. You can try out the exercises with just a handful of people, but many of them can work for dozens or even hundreds at once. They are not only designed for educational situations, like classrooms and workshops, but also for a lunch break at work or just playing around with friends.

The exercises in this book come out of my experiences as a game player and designer, and from more than three decades of teaching design. They have been played by artists, educators, students, technologists, businesspeople, researchers, and designers of all kinds—from kids in after-school programs to creative leads at the biggest game companies in the world. They are valuable for anyone who wants to know more about how people think, how systems work, how to create meaningful experiences, and how to redesign the world for the better.

A Ludic Century

Games and play are the vehicle for the ideas and experiences of this book, but they are not the destination. In other words, you can (and will!) devise wonderful play out of these exercises. But that's not the point. The point is what we can learn from games: how to be playfully flexible and creative, how to collaborate on problems, how to understand the parts of a complex system fitting together into a dynamic whole. These are key cognitive, social, and cultural skills. They are crucial aspects of being literate and engaged with the world today.

We are living at a time when so many aspects of our lives—the ways that we work and learn, how we communicate and socialize and romance, the ways that we engage with government and connect with our communities—are mediated by complex networks of information. Our lives are ruled by financial databases and social networks and vast bureaucracies of information that we will never see.

As part of this trend line, media, art, and entertainment are becoming increasingly modular, interactive, and customizable. The moving image has shifted from darkened cinemas and flickering television screens to the internet, to be endlessly streamed and sliced and shared. Information no longer comes from a set of encyclopedias on a shelf but instead from the participatory, evolving, contentious processes of Wikipedia. The rise of digital games as an economic and cultural powerhouse is both a cause and an effect of this shift. In fact, the twenty-first century might be termed a Ludic Century, an epoch in which games and play are the model for how we interact with culture and with each other.

This doesn't mean that in the future everything will be a game. It does mean that games are an important way of understanding these changes occurring across society and technology and design—because games have always been modular, interactive, customizable systems. Every game ever played, from five-thousand-year-old board games to last year's video game blockbusters, are situations in which people push and pull at inputs and outputs, exploring and inhabiting and manipulating. The ancient cultural form of games turns out to be a kind of miniature laboratory for practicing these emerging forms of twenty-first-century literacy.

And we need them more than ever. The problems of the Ludic Century are complex system problems. Environmental collapse, social inequity, the design of democracy itself—these seemingly intractable challenges are tied to our increasingly integrated and complicated world. I believe games can help. Not that playing itself solves these problems, but the kinds of thinking that come out of games and play are exactly the kinds of thinking that can begin to address these wicked challenges.

Craft + Culture

The exercises and ideas in this book engage with both the craft and the culture of design. They refine the craft by getting into the nitty-gritty specifics of things like brainstorming ideas, iterating through a rigorous process, and communicating with precision. At the same time, and perhaps even more importantly, they highlight the fact that design is always already culture. In other words: the meanings and impacts and values of design are connected to real-world people and contexts.

Let me use as an example my own home turf: designing games. Games are absolutely full of craft: the challenges of writing elegant rules or optimizing powerful code, the tricky pacing of telling an interactive story, the nuances of evolving a dynamic social economy. For too many designers, the buck stops there. What about larger cultural contexts? For instance, what about the environmental impact of games? The dimensions of a tabletop game box (often mostly empty air used to inflate the perceived value of the product) radically multiply its environmental footprint. And high-traffic online game servers and planned obsolescence of video game hardware make the digital game industry incredibly destructive to the planet.

Considering design as culture goes beyond environmental impact, of course. Consider, too, the politics of race, gender, or class that are embodied in the representations of a game. And consider how those politics are reflected (or not) in the companies and teams that are doing the designing. There are the labor economics that the manufacturing, distribution, and sale of a game help to perpetuate. And of course, none of these are isolated considerations. Climate, race, and economic justice are all deeply intertwined.

No design is an island. Being a designer is the challenge of being stretched in all of these directions at once. Be a hardcore snob of your craft. Be a warrior of design culture too. Honestly, what's the alternative?

Playing with Ideas

So what exactly can you learn from the exercises in this book? The pioneering computer scientist Seymour Papert famously called a concept a "thing to think with." To me that means learning is not about acquiring data but instead is about interacting with other people and the world. The exercises in this book are ways of practicing this kind of hands-on, experiential learning. Each exercise gives you new things to think with. A partial list:

A grounded sense of self. Playing is a way to feel loose and free in our bodies and minds. As we play, we come to know who we are and learn to experiment with new ways of being.

Analyzing how systems work. Understanding, modifying, and designing the intricate structures of games is a remarkably effective way of practicing systems thinking.

Understanding people. We design for other people, observing them throughout the design process. Play is a place to deepen our awareness of human psychology and emotions.

Communicating ideas. Games are artificial languages of meaning. Playing and designing them are occasions to practice the essential design skill of communication.

Flexible thinking. In game design, you sometimes think like a mathematician and at other times like a storyteller, or a party host, or an anthropologist. Playing stretches your mind in new ways.

Creative problem solving. As unpredictable complex systems, games force us to try out ideas, see what is and isn't working, and proceed through creative experimentation.

Productive collaboration. Whether you are playing with others, engaging with playtesters, or working with fellow designers, play requires constant collaborative activity.

Designing human experiences. Play and games engage every part of us, from our physical senses to our social and cultural selves. Designing for others is training in understanding people.

A rigorous process of making. The iterative game design process—the cycle of prototyping, playtesting, and analyzing—is a useful model for designing anything.

Critically connecting to culture. The meaning of play emerges from how we interact with the world. Games can be a place to play with the complex web of culture.

How is any of this relevant to what you do? That's a question only you can answer. Figuring out the value of something is best discovered as you explore that something. What's the purpose of a joke? Or a pencil? Or friendship?

Play and Systems and Design

The book is divided into three parts:

Play is about the messy, wild, creative improvisation of playing. More than just goofing around, play is a profound way of understanding how we relate to each other, how meaning is made, and how to critically engage with the world.

Exercises in Play are games that usually take half an hour or less to play and discuss. Many of them are physical, playground-style activities curated from traditional folk culture and contemporary designers. They are great for warming up bodies and brains while also highlighting fundamental questions about people and design.

Systems takes a close look at how the parts of a complex structure interrelate to form a whole. Systems thinking is a crucial kind of literacy, and games get right to the heart of interactive systems.

Exercises in Systems are mostly tabletop activities that take a couple of hours to work through. By analyzing, modifying, and tinkering with dynamic systems, these exercises train critical design skills that are widely applicable to just about any kind of complex project.

Design uses games as the occasion to practice inventing new ideas and projects. The emphasis is on rapid prototyping and iteration through playtesting—exploring ideas by actually making things and seeing how they work when you start to play with them.

Exercises in Design are longer projects that can stretch over days or weeks. They cover idea generation, working through a rigorous and playful process, and communicating to an audience. They are relevant to all kinds of creative endeavors.

Each section includes short essays—a few ways of thinking about play, or systems, or design. Each essay offers a different (and sometimes contradictory) lens on the core concepts of this book. You most definitely don't have to read them before you start playing around.

The game sheets at the end of the book contain pages to be photocopied that will help facilitate some of the exercises. TheRulesWeBreak.com contains online resources that can be used with the exercises, including digital versions of the game sheets. Please share and distribute the materials and the exercises widely.

One final request: don't just accept these exercises as they are. Make them your own. Play with them. Bend them. Break them. Transform them into something new. Please let me know how it all works out. I'm looking forward to hearing from you!

PLAY

It's a choice, this being in play, and to make
this choice you need to be aware that such
a gift is available to you and yours, all the time.

To play you don't need toys or costumes or joke
books. You don't even need games, although they
can help. But you do have to be open, vulnerable.
You do have to let go.

Play is all about that vulnerability, about being
responsive, yielding to the moment. You might not
be playing, but if you are willing to play, at the
drop of a hat, the bounce of a ball, the glance of
a toddler, the wag of a tail—then you are open to
any opportunity. You are loose. Responsive. Present.

Play means presence, but not just presence.
Responsiveness, but not just responsiveness.
Presence and responsiveness, lightness
and attentiveness, improvisation and creativity,
a willingness to let go and become part of
something new.

Bernard De Koven
The Infinite Playground

A FEW WAYS TO THINK ABOUT PLAY

PLAYING WITH SOMETHING

To play is to play
with something,
to question something
that might not
be meant for play
and to do something
inappropriately
playful with it.

Have you ever seen a kid who is walking playfully? Maybe hopping from foot to foot, or spinning around with each step, or walking dangerously backward without looking? Or perhaps the classic playful walk: doing anything possible not to step on sidewalk cracks? We immediately recognize these variations on ordinary walking as play. They all take a logical action—walking with a purpose, getting from point A to point B—and play with it.

Doodling on the back of a credit-card receipt. Humming along with the rhythm of a car alarm. Inventing funny nicknames for someone you love. Playing around. Playing in strange places. Playing with something you shouldn't. Play is an attitude, a sensibility, a way of being. It is not any particular behavior or experience; it is an approach to engaging with the world.

To play with something is to explore its possibilities, to test its limits, to move beyond the functional and utilitarian and into the realm of the unexpected and inappropriate. Punk rock played with the conventions of how to make music. Political revolutions play with the established order. New ideas play with old ideas. In experiencing play, we are training ourselves to be flexible and creative. To be critical. To not just accept things as they are. As we play with something, we start to understand it in new ways. Often, we even transform that something into something new.

Play is like a shamelessly generous parasite. It grabs on to other things—behaviors, objects, situations—but instead of sucking the life out of them, it does exactly the opposite. It enlivens them. It brings joy. It opens up potentials you never would ever have thought possible.

AGAINST THE RULES

Logical, rigid rules
are the very opposite
of unexpected,
creative play.
Yet we design play
by designing the
rules, out of which
play emerges.

Rules are the raw material of game design. Open a board game: What's inside? A deck of cards, a couple of dice, a game board, maybe some colorful pawns. Yet the rules of the game are what help you understand how to deploy these materials in play. Rules are the structural underbelly of games—the engine under the hood— that players enact to set a game in motion.

In most games, the rules need to be absolutely, completely clear to everyone—without exception. Imagine playing Baseball in a park and using a tree as second base. A player holding on to a branch of the tree is tagged out, and an argument begins. One team thought only the trunk was

second base, but the other team thinks it's the whole tree! Who is right? For the game to continue, this confusion needs to be resolved. Rules are funny this way. They insist on maximum clarity: rules are logical, fixed, and unambiguous. What does it mean when my token lands on a red square? I don't know—let's look it up in the rules. To play a game, you must follow the rules and submit to their authority. From this point of view, games don't sound like much fun. *Enter my dictatorship of rules and obey!*

But that's not the way it works. When you actually begin a game and decide to limit your behavior to the restrictions dictated by the rules, what happens is play. And play is the opposite of rules. While rules are fixed and rigid and logical, play is unpredictable and spontaneous and creative. This is a deep and profound paradox. Play is everything rules are not—but at the same time, is dependent on and emerges out of rules.

This same relationship—a rigid structure that results in unexpected spontaneity—appears in all kinds of systems and situations. The designed structures of a building limit how people can move but cannot ever predict the romantic encounters or late-night parties that may happen inside. The rules of English grammar structure the possibilities of language but could not alone result in a poem by Emily Dickinson or the front page of the *New York Times*.

Designers create structures—like the rules of a game. Through an almost magical process, these structures wind up producing play. The trick is helping beautiful play bloom out of the raw materials of rules. This happens when you pay attention not just to the rules themselves but to the whole situation. Who is playing your game, and why? What are their expectations and states of mind as they begin? What might encourage your players to engage with and embrace the rules—just enough—so that they melt away into the jouissance of play?

FREE MOVEMENT

Play is free movement within a more rigid structure. Like a loose gear, the wiggling movement of play happens because of, but also in opposition to, the logical systems on which it depends.

You can act in a play. Or play the radio. One of my favorite uses of *play* in English is when we are talking about the loose movement of a gear or a steering wheel. That little wobble of movement is called play or free play.

In *Rules of Play* (2004), designer and researcher Katie Salen Tekinbaş and I defined play as "free movement within a more rigid structure." The play of the steering wheel exists only because of logical, utilitarian systems: the axle, drive shaft, and other parts that help the car move. Yet the play also exists *despite* those structures. The play —the extra back-and-forth wiggle when the steering wheel is not actually turning the tires— is the exact moment when the system is not doing something purely logical and utilitarian. The play exists in the spaces between—the interstices where the system is not doing its prescribed job.

Play is playing with and between structures. Playing Stoop Ball (1930s) on the front steps, you play with gravity and your body, enjoying how it feels to catch and to throw a ball. You also play with architectural functionality, turning a stairway stoop into a playfield. Maybe the bouncing ball is interrupting sidewalk traffic or someone's nap and thereby playing against the rules of proper behavior. Stoop Ball happens because of functional structures, like a front stoop. At the very same time, you are playing against the intended use of those structures.

But play goes way beyond just wiggling between fixed structures. Play has transformational potential: the free movement actually changes the foundational structures themselves. Language evolves like this. The meaning of the word *gamer* has shifted over the last few decades from indicating an antisocial nerd to being reclaimed as a positive term of game-playing pride to the more recent negative connotation of a toxic video game fan. As culture and usage shift, new forms of language emerge, spread within a culture, and are adopted as a new standard. By that point, new meanings have already begun to bubble up in the margins. Language is a cultural ecosystem that is constantly in a state of dynamic transformation.

Play is a way of thinking about this kind of transformational change. Play is the free movement that just might shift the rigid structures of society. For the designer of such revolutionary movements, the paradox is that you can't directly design the outcomes of play. You establish rules and structures—with the hope that they will become agents of transformation. Sometimes they do, sometimes they don't. Making play is an experiment in how we can change the world.

SOMETHING TO DO

Play is not content: it is an *activity*. Designing playful experiences means creating moments of meaningful participation— in the immediate moment and also in the long term.

Media, art, and entertainment are changing. They are becoming less about reading or watching or listening—the consumption of images and information—and more about active participation. This shift goes by many names: *linear* versus *interactive* or *lean back* versus *lean forward*. By whatever name, there is no doubt that we engage with media today through participation— streaming on multiple devices, sharing our reactions on social media, downloading and remixing and posting online.

Games are particularly helpful reference points for this shift. For centuries, games have never been about passive observation. Games have always been *something to do*. This kind of participatory experience goes beyond telling a story or creating content. It is designing an activity, an activity that can fill minutes, hours, days, or even years of someone's life. It means designing moments when somebody acts and something happens as a result. And it also means stringing those isolated moments together into a larger experience. You need to design with both timescales in mind: the immediate moment-to-moment as well as the long-term trajectory.

Game designers use the term *core mechanic* to talk about the main play activity of a game. A dirty little secret of game design is that most games are pretty repetitive. In UNO (1971), all you do is draw cards into your hand and then play those cards on the table. In *Fortnight* (2017), you mostly run and shoot, pick up equipment, and run and shoot some more. The same atoms of activity, over and over again. How do these simple actions become so meaningful?

The core mechanic should be intrinsically satisfying—it's fun to reveal a hidden card or explore virtual terrain. Yet all by themselves, these instants of interaction would quickly wear thin. What gives these actions staying power— what makes these moments meaningful over time—is context. A game provides a designed situation in which the primitive atom of the core mechanic can be combined to create new molecules of meaning.

In UNO, the cards on the table, your current hand, and the larger social rhythms of the game ("Play your Skip card so Chris loses a turn!") all provide context that gives meaning to each card you draw and play. In *Fortnight*, the shrinking island playfield, competition on the leaderboards, custom-downloaded dance moves, your favorite streamer's sarcastic in-jokes all give meaning to the core activity of the game, whether you're playing or spectating.

Designers of participatory experiences need to think about an engaging core mechanic. They also need to think about the context in which that moment-to-moment activity becomes meaningful. This is a different way of being a designer—less like a content creator and more like a party host. Less about making beautiful images or telling profound stories (although those are still just as important!) and more about structuring human behavior in ways that lead to meaningful give-and-take, as people take part in something to do.

The lesson? When you're designing, the tendency is to spend a lot of time discussing ideas and concepts. Instead, *design by doing*. Get to the point where you are making something interactive as soon as possible. Don't talk about a story: tell a story. Don't theorize about the experience: actually build it. Put together a prototype. Exercise your ability to play.

BEING SOMEONE ELSE

Play lets us try out new identities. Moving between and among the individual layers of person, player, and character is a powerful way that play can engage us.

In play we often take on new roles and personas. I might be the board game baroness of a mighty railroad empire, at war with my fellow industrialist players. Or a stealthy video game ninja seeking revenge on her enemies, who I puppet by pressing buttons on a controller. Through games we get to try out new versions of ourselves—sometimes aspirational, sometimes transgressive. Play is a context in which identities can be discovered, explored, and evolved. Even in games that might seem abstract, identities proliferate. On a soccer team, you might be given a position to play (forward), a role on the squad (assistant captain), a historical identity (the same jersey number as Abby Wambach), a professional identity (labor-agitating employee), or even the protagonist in a media narrative (up-and-coming prodigy).

Folklorist Gary Allen Fine, in his book *Shared Fantasies* (1983), distilled three distinct layers on which identity operates for participants in role-playing games like Dungeons and Dragons (1974). There is the layer of the *character* in the game, who is expressed when the players take action in the game world or speak in the voice of their fictional persona. There is the layer of *player*,

as we manage statistics and roll dice, trying to outsmart the game master and accumulate points for the next level. Finally, the layer of *person*, with relationships and responsibilities outside of the game: Whose turn is it to pay for the pizza? Why aren't there more girls in our game club? Playing a game doesn't mean occupying just one of these layers. It means existing on all of them at the same time. Flickering between and among these levels *is* play. Play can play with identity too.

This is the problem with notions of "immersion," which tend to assume game players somehow leave the real world behind and lose themselves completely in virtual worlds and characters. In an arcade fighting game, on one level you identify with the character you're playing, extending yourself into the world of the game. You also exist as a player, studying the quirks of the game, looking for tiny advantages, trying to outthink your opponent's moves, trash talking to rattle her nerves. At the same time, as a person in an arcade, you navigate the social hierarchy of the local gamer scene or strategize how to maximize the value of the quarters you put into the machine. This fluctuating play of identity is what immersion really is.

On the reality show *Manor House* (2002), a middle-class British family role-plays as landed Edwardian gentry, along with others who play their servants. What happens on the show is remarkable. In a few short weeks, the family, truly immersed in the material and social conditions of Edwardian England, begins to take on the class consciousness of the period. The father says and believes things that seem outrageous to our modern ears: that the members of the family deserve to have been born to this way of life or that their servants genuinely love them. (In fact, the participants playing the demanding "servant" roles were on the brink of leaving the show.)

Immersion in a fictional world of play is also immersion into an ideological reality. This is because player identities exist simultaneously in the artificial world of the game and also in the real world. We play with and against these identities as we discover who we are—and who we might become through play.

COLLABORATIVE CONFLICT

Every game is based on a struggle of some kind. These conflicts embody a complex play of meaning, and the artifice of a game can sometimes spill into the real world.

A game is a conflict. That's true whether two teams are facing off for a Basketball (1891) game, a handful of friends are role-playing around a kitchen table, or you are absorbed in your latest smartphone puzzle addiction. Every game pits players, with or against each other, within a system of conflict.

Conflict might sound negative, like some kind of antagonistic competition. In fact, the conflict in games is always in some way collaborative. This is because everyone participating agrees, voluntarily, to take part in the game together. (If we're being forced to play, it's not really play.) We all decide to spend the next couple of minutes —or hours, or weeks—within the space of play and together keep the struggle of the game going. Even when we play alone, we are in a sense collaborating as part of a community of players who are all playing the same game.

The ongoing struggle of games weaves energy and engagement into the experience. When we play, we are taking part in productive conflict, joyful conflict, meaningful conflict. Conflict is part of the dramatic machinery of a game that grips our minds and emotions. As every storyteller knows, there is no drama without conflict. Conflict is the spark that helps games catch fire in us.

Part of the fear that games sometimes evoke— for example, the fear of violence from violent video games—comes from a misunderstanding of our relationship to the conflict inherent in games. When we play a game, we do not become confused about whether or not the game is real. In fact, we are able to lose ourselves in play because (paradoxically!) we know that games are artificial. The conflict in games is like two actors fighting on a stage—an artificial, theatrical combat. The audience members watching from their seats don't rush up on stage to intervene and stop the fight. Instead, they sit in the theater and suspend their disbelief. They can be gripped by the drama of the fight—yet at the same time, also know that it's artificial.

All of this happens on the very atomic level of play. In his essay "A Theory of Play and Fantasy" (1955), philosopher Gregory Bateson observed that when a dog nips another dog—when it gives a play-bite—it is communicating two things. The nip means "I am biting you" (a kind of signifier for a bite), yet a nip simultaneously also means "I am not biting you, I am just playing." Even dogs, in a sense, suspend their disbelief. When we take part in the artificial conflict of play, we are taking part in this multilayered metaconsciousness.

Nonetheless, play can sometimes go wrong. Occasionally, play-fighting dogs slip into real fighting. Perhaps a moment of panic escalates, and suddenly the growls and bites get real as the collaborative spirit of playing together is shattered by real fighting. The fragile, artificial conflict of games can bleed into reality, in very unpleasant ways. Video games all too often can be breeding grounds for the worst kinds of online culture, in which marginalized players find themselves attacked. "It's just a game" doesn't hold water when play becomes abusive. These toxic patterns—dehumanizing trolling, winning at all costs, biased harassment—are the antithesis of playing well together.

This is the double-edged potential of conflict. How do you maintain collaborative play in the midst of full-tilt struggle? How do you harness the elemental spark of dramatic conflict without letting it burn down the whole game? How does conflict resist toxicity and remain productive, meaningful, and joyful?

A SOCIAL CONTRACT

When we play,
a special kind of
community springs
up. We all agree
to play together
and to change the
rules if we want.

In *The Moral Judgment of the Child* (1932), psychologist Jean Piaget traced the ways that children come to understand the rules of the game Marbles. In his native Switzerland, Piaget found that the way kids played the game was extremely local. Different rules for chalking a circle, shooting your marbles, capturing opponents (and sometimes keeping them!) varied from town to town and neighborhood to neighborhood. These rules were purely children's culture, traditions passed down from older to younger kids, free of adult interference or the commercialization of today's mass media.

Piaget found that children move through three different stages as they learn how to play Marbles. The youngest kids have a vague sense that there are rules you are supposed to follow, but they don't quite understand how they work. They will play *at* the game of Marbles, drawing a circle in the sand and maybe knocking a marble or two, but not fully comprehend the entire system.

In the second stage, usually starting around age five, children are able to understand the rules of Marbles and fully play the game—but in a very particular way. They hold the rules as a kind of sacred authority. They play strictly by the rules only and won't permit any bending or breaking of them. There is only one right way to play the game.

The third stage begins around age ten. Children come to see Marbles as a social contract, a set of rules that gain their authority only because the players agree to follow them. This means that if everyone agrees, the rules can be changed. This is essentially how adults see games too: as a voluntary, social construct. Play in this sense is wonderfully flexible but also quite fragile. Play happens only if and when we all agree to it.

Game designer Bernie DeKoven viewed this kind of play community as a space for gaining a truer understanding of oneself. In his book *The Well-Played Game* (1978), he describes the power of realizing that players can change the game if they want—in order to all play better together. This is not gratuitous disruption for its own sake. It is deep play that blurs the lines between players and designers. It challenges us to be more sensitive and open to each other. It requires active attention to the needs of others in the moment of play.

For Piaget, the game of Marbles was a lens for exploring how our morals develop. For DeKoven, the play community is a chance to practice being better people together. These are not just abstract ideas. Every moment of play is an opportunity to exercise collaboration with other human beings and to explore the curious social contract of play.

SECOND-ORDER SURPRISES

Play is a second-order design problem. You can't design play directly—you only design the circumstances under which it might arise.

Designing a playful experience is less like making a beautiful object—and more like building a box of tools. Players will take whatever you designed and construct their own experiences with it, experiences that can't be fully anticipated in advance. This can be scary! But it is also why play is so powerful.

The rules of a game will never describe everything that happens in the game. In Poker (early 1800s), there are no rules for bluffing. Bluffing is an emergent behavior that arises out of other structures—the fact that your cards are hidden from opponents, the progressive rounds of betting, the importance of deceiving your opponents about the strength of your hand. Bluffing is not explicitly mentioned in the rules of Poker, but it is the center around which the entire game revolves.

SiSSYFiGHT 2000 (1999) is a multiplayer online game I designed with Word.com. Everyone is a little girl on a playground, trying to survive with their self-esteem intact. Each turn, you pick an action like tattling or teasing or licking your lolly—all while text chatting with other players. How each turn plays out depends on the actions everyone chose. (Teasing only works if two or more girls teased the same target; tattling gets everyone else in trouble—but if two players tattle, the tattlers are punished.) Inspired by game theory and social tabletop games, it is a darkly humorous design that encourages playful backstabbing and deceit.

The rules of *SiSSYFiGHT 2000* are fairly simple, but the play that emerged was surprising. Players invented all kinds of "house rules"— variations that challenged them to play in new ways, such as outlawing tattles or playing "silent treatment" games in which chatting was not allowed. Some players creatively figured out how to cheat—by double-sessioning and playing two characters in two different browsers at once. Almost immediately a response emerged in the form of a culture of online vigilantes. These do-gooders published "How to Spot a Cheater" guides and roamed the playgrounds with lists of known violators to stamp out this breach of community etiquette.

The *SiSSYFiGHT 2000* team did not directly design any of these surprises. We only set the initial structures in place, helped evolve the community, and celebrated playful creativity when it did happen. The sweetest pleasure of design is seeing your audience do things you never could have possibly anticipated. This is the second-order nature of play design: you establish the rules, but the players take it from there. It is a chance to humble your sense of authorship by sharing it with your audience. Rather than expressing your own ideas, can your design be a place where players express themselves?

GAMES OF DESIRE

Systems of play embody the curious contradictions of pleasure. We take on unnecessary obstacles to perpetuate a dance with our own libidos.

Consider, for a moment, the playground classic Tag. When you are playing Tag, what are you doing? Trying to stay away from whoever is It, of course. Desperately, you do whatever you can to run away from them—giggling, dodging, running.

And then something happens—a sudden misstep, a flailing arm—and you get tagged. Then you are It. And everything changes. Suddenly you are the shunned loner. Or perhaps it feels more like being a demonic monster whose very touch causes instant death—as the mortals flee helplessly from you! You chase the others—giggling, dodging, running—until one of them is tagged, becomes It, and the game continues.

This entire looping system—of running bodies, of players desperate to touch each other, of predators and prey swapping places, of energy rising and falling and flowing—is a system of desire. What do Tag players want? To be pursued, to escape, to hunt, and to kill. To be captured, to be free, to keep playing. To have fun.

All games partake of desire, in a thousand different ways. Video games seduce our brains with loot boxes and thrill our imaginations with high-res power fantasies. Role-playing games transport us willingly into co-constructed fictions.

Sports push us to compete in emotion-laden contests with opponents who are also our intimate collaborators.

As we play, we are playing with our own sense of ourselves. We willingly take on challenges and frustrations, just so that we can enjoy them. Philosopher Bernard Suits has called this playful impulse for unnecessary obstacles the "ludic attitude." In *Grasshopper: Games, Life, and Utopia* (1978), he observes that if you really wanted to get a Golf ball into a hole, you wouldn't stand a huge distance away, put trees and sand traps between yourself and the hole, and limit yourself to hitting it with a stick. Yet that is exactly what we do, because people play Golf (1400s). Desire is constituted by contradictions that defy rational sense.

In play, we instrumentalize our own desire. The artificial challenges of games become a kind of mirror. They create a space where we can externalize our wishes and fears and pleasure and pain. In these contexts we come to know ourselves in new ways. *Ten Meter Tower* (2016), a documentary short by Maximilien van Aertryck and Axel Danielson, films a series of people at the top of a high-diving platform. Alone and in pairs, they bargain and cajole, debate and lambaste themselves and each other about whether they can overcome their fear and jump off.

The film captures perfectly the way in which games perch us vertiginously on the edge of our own desire. We play with dangerous possibility, tease our own egos, dance with a primal version of ourselves. Every game is like a miniature version of the famous (and famously debunked) marshmallow test, in which a child is left alone with one marshmallow and told that they will get a second marshmallow—if they can endure the wait. Like the children squirming against their desire to eat a marshmallow in exchange for more pleasure later on, play is a crucible where we bargain in suffering and reward.

To design play is to celebrate and grapple with these very human contradictions. There is no final winning state to Tag. It is a perpetual motion machine of desire that never has to end. A game begins, is nurtured like a communal magic ritual, and rolls forward through constant transformation. Until it stops and a different game begins—or perhaps no game at all.

UNWRITTEN RULES

There is more to play than just the logical rules of the game. We also play by invisible social rules. Who gets included in play and who is left out?

The rules of a game are bigger than you might think. What are the rules of Tic-Tac-Toe? You need a three-by-three grid; two players alternate taking turns, putting an X or O into an empty square; three in a row is a win. Lastly, if no one can play, it's a draw.

But there are other, *unwritten* rules too. What about how much time you take on your turn? What if, just when you were about to lose a game, instead of making a move you decide to think about it for a while. A long while. An hour. A week. A year. You wouldn't be violating any of the mathematical rules of Tic-Tac-Toe. However, you would be defying the spirit of the game and a commonly understood sense of what it means to sit down for a quick match.

There are plenty of other unwritten rules too. Can you tickle your opponent so they can't make a move? Or bribe them to let you win? There are innumerable situations that will never be fully covered by the logical rules of the game. As philosopher Stephen Sniderman writes about in "Unwritten Rules" (1999), to play with another person isn't just about the particular game you are playing. You are always playing with them in some larger social context. When we play a game, we

aren't just following the written rules, we are also beholden to these unwritten social and cultural rules that guide our thinking and interaction.

Outside of games, layers of written and unwritten rules structure our lives too. Who is stopped by airport security? Which parent postpones their career to raise a child? Which spouse takes care of an ailing parent? Sometimes rules—written and unwritten—set people free to play with each other. At least as often, they do the opposite—reinforce bias and power imbalance.

Games are occasions to practice a critical relationship to rules. Everything that this book is about—being loose and playful and creative, understanding rules in order to break them, redesigning systems of inequity for the better—can only happen when more of us play. An exercise in play can be a moment to set aside the worries of the world for an experience of joyful release. At the same time, it can also be a chance to sharpen our critical understanding of why and how play happens. Who gets to play? Who has the privilege to join the game or to break the rules? Who is included and who is left out?

A design will always bump into unwritten rules. If you are making use of these exercises, pay attention to the unwritten rules of the situation you are helping to create, so that everyone can feel comfortable and playful together. Can you make things inclusive for everyone? Can you give space for those who don't want to play? Or, even better, change the game to let more people in? Keying into the unwritten rules can help us embrace a more expansive idea of play— and a more expansive sense of ourselves and of each other.

INSIGHTFUL TRANSGRESSIONS

Play is a model for critical engagement. Playing with existing structures is a strategy for questioning and reconfiguring the rules of our lives outside of games.

If play always plays with something, it can also make that something into something else. We learn rules but only so that they can be understood, analyzed, questioned, bent, broken, discarded, and refashioned into something new. Play means playing where we are not supposed to be playing. Doing what we are not supposed to be doing. Play is that which doesn't quite fit. Play is the devilish trick, the hack to the system, but with the purpose of making a better play community for everyone.

Inside of games, play often lets us do things that we couldn't do in ordinary life. In the cutthroat board game Diplomacy (1954), it's only a matter of time before you backstab your friends. In Boxing (late 1800s), two athletes pummel each other in ways that would get them arrested outside the ring. So what happens when we take play outside of games?

The artists The Yes Men printed and distributed 80,000 fake issues of the *New York Times* in 2008. They played with the real structures of the paper (typography, writing style, physical format) to invent fictional utopian stories, like the end of the Iraq War and an overhaul of the tax system that finally eliminates poverty. The hoax edition, given away for free at busy transit stations, fooled many New Yorkers.

In Adrian Piper's 1986 artwork *My Calling Card*, when someone in Piper's life made or laughed at or agreed with a racist remark, Piper would hand them a business card. The card informs the reader that Piper is Black (although she sometimes passes for being white) and includes the following: "I regret any discomfort my presence is causing you, just as I am sure you regret the discomfort your racism is causing me." Playing with and between the structures of racial identity and polite conversation, Piper's piece points out social structures that perpetuate racism. It is a bracingly playful work.

My Calling Card and the hoaxed *New York Times* are playing where they are not supposed to be playing and doing things they are not supposed to be doing. These active forms of critical engagement do more than just convey a message. In how they engage with culture, they embody a kind of design research through play, highlighting what exists through mischievous processes that also point to what and how things might change for the better.

Play can be a way of critically engaging with the world. As you play a game, ask: Who is allowed the privilege of playing in this space? What rules are being followed? Who gets to break them? As you design play, ask: What kind of play are you trying to engender? How does your play fit into where it is taking place? What do you hope will happen as a result? To play is to investigate these questions. To play is to transgress productively; to produce insight and also transformation; to uncover playful ways of being; to find new ways of playing together.

EXERCISES
WHEN YOU HAVE 20–30 MINUTES TO PLAY

FIVE FINGERS

Point at someone and they
lose a finger—5 fingers
gone and they're out!
A very simple game
of intense social politics
that demonstrates how
play creates meaning.

1. Divide into groups

Form into groups of about 6 players each.
Groups do not need to have the same number
of players. Groups of a dozen or more work
well too—it will just take a little longer to play.
This exercise can work with hundreds of people
all playing at the same time.

2. Explain how to play

I like to explain Five Fingers like this:

> Hold out 1 hand with all 5 fingers outstretched.
> These 5 fingers are extremely important. They
> are your life! When you lose all of your fingers,
> you are out of the game and you can only watch.
>
> Someone in the group starts, and you take turns
> going around the circle. When it is your turn,
> you do one thing and one thing only: with your
> other hand, you point at someone else in the
> circle. That person loses a finger.

Demonstrate your outstretched hand going
down from 5 to 4 fingers.

> And that's it! Keep going around the circle taking
> turns. When you lose all of your fingers, you
> are out of the game. The last remaining player
> is the winner. Any questions?

Think about: Enjoying the rules

I used to hurry through explaining the rules of a game
like Five Fingers, with the idea of getting everyone
playing as quickly as possible. I have learned from
grandmaster of play Bernie DeKoven to slow down
and enjoy the performance of explaining rules. Take
your time. Be clear and repeat key ideas. Make jokes.
Build suspense. Have fun.

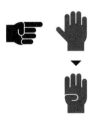

What You Need

■ Any number of players,
in person or remote online

■ 15 minutes

What You Learn

◆ Complex meaning emerges from
simple rules

◆ Games can be a context for playfully
cruel social interaction

◆ Creative play happens within
structured systems

FIVE FINGERS

3. Play!

Then let them play. Participants may be skeptical at first, but as soon as they get rolling, you will start hearing squeals of nervous laughter erupting across the room.

Wander among the groups of players, and make sure there aren't any questions as people start playing. Some groups may play much more carefully and slowly than others. Fast groups can start a second game, and slower groups can be urged to hurry up and finish. Definitely let everyone get to the end! Committing ludus interruptus would not be a good idea. When the last group finishes up, thank everyone for playing and have everyone in the room give themselves a round of applause.

Think about: Observing play

As the groups play, take note of what they do. Look for examples of creative play: people celebrating their own deaths, dramatic full-body pointing attacks, or using the (ahem!) middle finger to indicate only having one life left. I have seen groups vote democratically on who should be eliminated or even—my absolute favorite!—a group that agreed to stop playing because they didn't want to exclude anyone.

4. Talk about what happened

So much complicated play comes out of such an elemental set of rules! Five Fingers demonstrates in miniature the powerful forces of play that can be unleashed when players all agree to step into the context of a game and play with each other.

Discuss: What is the relationship between the rules and the play of Five Fingers?

Five Fingers engenders intense, engaged play. Players quickly move from learning a set of logical rules to making spontaneous emotional outbursts. Right from the start, the rules of Five Fingers force players to choose a target and engage in a bitter contest of survival. The rules are so simple! But as the play reverberates through the group of players, each decision becomes complex.

Discuss: What are examples of creative play that happened?

Were there any unexpected improvisations that happened during a game? You can share your observations and ask players to report what they saw. Games are situations in which we don't just play *in* a system, we also play *with* the system. Rules facilitate play, but players make it their own.

For remote play

Five fingers works well in a video chat or in breakout rooms. Everyone holds up 5 fingers to the camera, and when it is your turn, rather than pointing, you name your target. Because you're not all sitting in a circle, you can change the turn order rule so that the person just targeted is the one who takes the next turn. (If they just perished, they pick another player to go next.) This actually makes the revenge politics even more intense!

Context

Five Fingers is inspired by the "chip-taking game" thought experiment from the highly recommended book *Characteristics of Games* (2012), by Richard Garfield, Robert Gutchera, and Skaff Elias. The original version uses piles of chips instead of fingers, but the "pure politics" elimination gameplay is the same. Five Fingers is a fantastic icebreaker to play in a classroom or when giving a talk to a very large room. Because it's so easy to learn and so intensely social, it's a devilishly fun way to open a discussion on a number of fundamental topics.

Discuss: How does Five Fingers create meaning out of player actions?

In games we create and exchange meaning. Pointing in real life can mean a lot of different things, but Five Fingers gives pointing a context that adds layers of significance. You point at someone in Five Fingers and bring them one step closer to banishment and death. Or perhaps pointing just invites retaliation and revenge back at you! The rules of games are a kind of conversational grammar—players use that grammar to create meaning and express themselves to each other.

Discuss: Is Five Fingers a mean or antisocial game? Or is it perhaps the opposite?

Often in play we can do things that are not permitted outside the game, such as mercilessly attacking a friend (or a stranger) in a board game or boxing ring. Five Fingers is a deeply social game of pure politics, in which strategies revolve around emotions and psychology more than math and logic. It can be quite cruel—in a very playful way. Enjoyment of the game comes in part from ducking the angry mob, riding out the waves of recriminations, and somehow surviving all the way to the end.

ZEN COUNTING

Everyone closes their eyes. People count out numbers from 1 to 10—but if 2 people count at the same time, the group starts over. Zen Counting is a meditative experience of intuitive cooperation.

1. Settle into place

Zen Counting works best when everyone is feeling quiet and relaxed. The game works with as few as 3 players, and up to a dozen or so (if you have more people than that, split into multiple groups). The members of a group should be near each other, but it's best if they are not sitting in a regular arrangement (like chairs in a circle). Lying on backs or sitting on the floor in a semirandom scatter works very well.

2. Explain how to play

Have everyone take a few deep breaths. Then talk everyone through these rules:

> Close your eyes and keep them closed as you play. Whosoever feels so moved can begin by counting out loud, starting with "1." Anyone else can then continue the count by saying "2." And then "3," and so on. One important rule— the same person can't count twice in a row. So if you count "3,"someone else has to say "4" before you can count again. Now here's the twist. If 2 people say a number at the same time—if their count overlaps even just a little bit—then the group has to start over from the number 1 again. Can you count to 10?

3. Play a few times

If there are no questions, each group can start playing. If a group makes it to 10, see if they can reach 20. Or even further. It may take a few tries for a group to find their rhythm and get past 3 or 4. Or they might hit on a pattern and be able to continue indefinitely.

4. Share your experience

Zen Counting is a subtly nuanced form of play. You can choose to discuss it or not. Sometimes the experience of the exercise itself is enough, and talking about it spoils the magic. It's OK to just sit in the afterglow of Zen Counting for a moment and not say anything at all.

What You Need

- 3 or more players, in person or remotely online
- 10 minutes

What You Learn

- Designing unexpected sensory experiences
- Cooperation that emerges from playful interaction
- A peaceful experience of finding group cohesion

SOCIAL PLAY

ZEN COUNTING

For remote play

Zen Counting's minimal design translates well to a video experience. Or even just an audio conference call. If there are a lot of people, try breakout rooms or have a subset of participants demonstrate a game while others watch. There might be a bit of a timing lag, which makes the overlapping counting even more challenging to avoid.

Context

Zen Counting comes from *The Infinite Playground* (2020) by Bernie DeKoven and Holly Gramazio, where it is presented as a meditative way to harmonize with others through play. Zen Counting is a quick and effective warm-up activity to get everyone in a collaborative spirit and to explore unconventional social interaction. For a similar and slightly more complicated experience, try Wolfgang Warsch's intriguing collaborative card game The Mind (2018).

Discuss: What just happened?

One place to start a discussion is to have participants simply share their experience of the game. Did it induce nail-biting anxiety? Exciting hive-mind collaboration? Or relaxing meditation? Contrasts between different participants are especially instructive.

Discuss: What about the design of Zen Counting creates a meditative experience?

Playing Zen Counting means paying careful attention to others and listening to the silences between numbers. Games can have us enact all kinds of activities: acting dramatically, solving mental puzzles, sprinting at top speed. Zen Counting offers something quite different.

Discuss: Did any creative rule bending or breaking take place?

Was there a group that settled into fixed counting patterns? Did some individuals refrain from counting altogether? Did anyone give out secret signals? Are these examples of rule bending positive ways to play creatively—or do they go against the intended spirit of the game? Who gets to decide? Each group of Zen Counting players intuitively evolves its own miniature social contract. It's fascinating to see how differently different groups can play.

WOLVES AND SHEEP

An exercise in cooperative competition. Each turn, choose: Are you a Wolf or a Sheep? The survival of the group depends on what everyone picked.

WOLVES AND SHEEP

What You Need

- Groups of 5–7 players, around tables
- 30 minutes
- 10–20 tokens per player (poker chips, small cubes, etc.)
- Game sheet, page 41

What You Learn

- Designing cooperation and competition
- A game as a kind of social contract
- The application of game theory to game design

1. Setup

Divide into groups of 5 to 7 players and have each group sit around a table. Place a big pile of tokens at the middle of each table. The tokens will be used to keep score. Prepare a copy of the rules handout of Wolves and Sheep for each group but don't pass it out just yet.

2. A sample game

Before they see what will happen, have each group play a single round. Tell them to secretly decide in their heads if they want to be:

- a Wolf (a fist), or
- a Sheep (a flat hand)

They don't know what that means yet, but that's OK. On the count of "1, 2, 3, go!" everyone simultaneously reveals their hand symbol to the rest of the group. Then pass out the rules sheet. It tells players how to score each round:

If your group is half or more Wolves, it is a "lean pack."

- get 2 points if you are a Wolf
- get 0 points if you are a Sheep

If your group is more than half Sheep, it is a "predator feast."

- get 5 points if you are a Wolf
- get 3 points if you are a Sheep

Each group can see whether they had a lean pack or a predator feast and what that means for each individual player. Players then take tokens from the stack on their table to keep track of their score.

Have players go through 3 more turns, and see who finished with the most points. Most players will end up as Wolves—it's definitely what the design encourages players to do.

WOLVES

Each turn:

Silently decide if you are a Sheep or a Wolf.

On the count of 3, hold out a fist if you are a Wolf or an open hand if you are a Sheep.

Keep your hands out— count the number of Wolves and Sheep in your group.

Keep score:

If your group is half or more Wolves, it is a "lean pack."

- 2 points if you are a Wolf
- 0 points if you are a Sheep

If your group is more than half Sheep, it is a "predator feast."

- 5 points if you are a Wolf
- 3 points if you are a Sheep

WOLVES

Each turn:

Silently decide if you are a Sheep or a Wolf.

On the count of 3, hold out a fist if you are a Wolf or an open hand if you are a Sheep.

Keep your hands out— count the number of Wolves and Sheep in your group.

Keep score:

If your group is half or more Wolves, it is a "lean pack."

- 2 points if you are a Wolf
- 0 points if you are a Sheep

If your group is more than half Sheep, it is a "predator feast."

- 5 points if you are a Wolf
- 3 points if you are a Sheep

WOLVES

Each turn:

Silently decide if you are a Sheep or a Wolf.

On the count of 3, hold out a fist if you are a Wolf or an open hand if you are a Sheep.

Keep your hands out— count the number of Wolves and Sheep in your group.

Keep score:

If your group is half or more Wolves, it is a "lean pack."

- 2 points if you are a Wolf
- 0 points if you are a Sheep

If your group is more than half Sheep, it is a "predator feast."

- 5 points if you are a Wolf
- 3 points if you are a Sheep

WOLVES

Each turn:

Silently decide if you are a Sheep or a Wolf.

On the count of 3, hold out a fist if you are a Wolf or an open hand if you are a Sheep.

Keep your hands out— count the number of Wolves and Sheep in your group.

Keep score:

If your group is half or more Wolves, it is a "lean pack."

- 2 points if you are a Wolf
- 0 points if you are a Sheep

If your group is more than half Sheep, it is a "predator feast."

- 5 points if you are a Wolf
- 3 points if you are a Sheep

SOCIAL PLAY

WOLVES AND SHEEP

3. Winter is coming

They are going to play another game, but with a new wrinkle. A long cold winter is coming, and to survive, the group needs to gather a certain number of total points—but even then, not everyone will make it.

They are going to play the game with the same scoring system. But this time, it's going to be harder to win. Here are the new rules:

- If the total points of everyone in the group is equal to or greater than the number of players times 10, then the group has saved enough to get through the winter. (A group of 4 needs 40 points.) But there's another twist: only the 2 players with the most individual points actually survive and win the game.

- If the total points of all players is less than the number of players times 10, then no one survives the winter and everyone loses.

- If more than 2 players tie for the highest points, then everyone dies—regardless of the total group points.

Have each group play through 4 turns, using the same process as the first game. Remind everyone that they are free to discuss their votes— negotiation is part of the game!

4. Discuss what happened

Have every group share a bit of what occurred around each table. You are likely to get very different kinds of experiences and strategies, depending on the prevailing vibe of a particular group. There should be lots to talk about.

Discuss: Is Wolves and Sheep a cooperative or competitive game?

The structure of Wolves and Sheep is known as "coopetition"—the players have to work together for a group goal (the total needed to survive the winter), but there are still individual goals (the 2 players with the most points get to live). By putting these 2 goals at cross-purposes, the design creates a rich space of social interaction.

Discuss: What kind of social behavior does the design of the game encourage?

Wolves and Sheep forces players to work together and still look out for themselves. Because they can negotiate each round, what you do from turn to turn— wheeling and dealing, keeping or breaking your promises—actually matters. The community of the game evolves through each player's behavior, as reputations are made and social norms are established and then violated.

Discuss: What kinds of creative play happened?

Under the duress of social pressure, you may well see some very creative play—ruthless deception, bald-faced bribing, or even strategic coordination of everyone's votes to equally distribute points. The elegance of Wolves and Sheep is that even a very simple design can act to shape complex social relationships and behavior.

Context

Many designers are interested in creating cooperative games, and this exercise provides a model for having players work together while also keeping dramatic social tension in place. Inspired by the classic Prisoner's Dilemma problem from game theory, Wolves and Sheep was invented by game designer Naomi Clark. Another fantastic game of social negotiation is the brilliant and delightful Werewolf (sometimes called Mafia), designed by Dimitry Davidoff in 1986, which offers related design lessons about hidden information, cutthroat politics, and social gameplay. Werewolf doesn't require any special materials to play, and the game rules (along with oodles of variations) can be found online.

Wander about, secretly picking other people to be your sun and moon. When everyone maneuvers to line up their eclipse, unexpected things happen.

ECLIPSE

ECLIPSE

1. Begin walking around

Eclipse is best played in a large room or area where people have plenty of space to meander around. To begin, just ask everyone to start walking. You can tell them:

> Begin wandering about, staying loose and relaxed. Take a few deep breaths in and out. Feel your body with each step as you walk. Sense the ground under you, the space around you, and everyone else walking around.

2. Play the game

Once they have settled into walking, tell them to keep moving as you explain the game:

> As you keep walking, you are going to secretly pick a Sun. Find someone else in the room and decide that they are your own personal Sun. Without revealing who you selected, enjoy basking in the rays of your Sun as you move about the space—be aware of where they are at all times as you continue wandering around.

Let them keep wandering for a moment—and then continue:

> Next, you are going to secretly pick a Moon. Find a different person in the room to be your Moon. Without letting anyone know, keep your Sun and your Moon in mind as you keep walking about.

Give them a few more moments of wandering:

> And now for the tricky part—you are going to make an eclipse. You are the Earth. A lunar eclipse happens when the moon comes directly between the sun and the earth. So as you keep wandering, you want to maneuver into place so that your Moon is located directly between you and your Sun. Are you ready? OK, make your eclipse happen!

And watch the chaos ensue.

What You Need

- A half dozen to a hundred players, in a room with lots of space
- 15 minutes

What You Learn

- Emergent complexity arises out of simple rules
- Designing physical experiences that are also social systems
- Players inhabit systems in creative ways

3. End the game and discuss what happened

After several minutes, when everyone has had a good go at it, start a final countdown from 10. The game ends when the countdown reaches 0—everyone freezes into place wherever they are.

As the game's final step, everyone can reveal who they selected as their Sun and Moon. On the count of 3, have them point at their Sun and Moon with each hand. If their arms are lined up and pointing together, they did manage to make an eclipse!

Then discuss. There is a lot going on under the hood of this simple game!

Discuss: What are the parts of Eclipse, and how do they interact with each other?

Systems are parts that interrelate in a context to form a whole. In a complex system, the parts don't have a static, fixed relationship; instead, they have dynamic, shifting relationships to other parts. The parts of Eclipse are the bodies of the players, and every time you move to try and better align your Sun and Moon, you are simultaneously affecting all the interrelationships.

Discuss: How does Eclipse demonstrate emergent complexity?

When you move, the alignments of other sets of Earths and Suns and Moons all change—giving rise to network effects that multiply and shift and change as everyone continually adjusts their positions. Remind everyone that what they actually did—the running around, or careful strategizing, or pleading and cajoling—was not described in any way within the rules of the game. These unexpected patterns are emergent complexity—unpredictable behavior that arises out of complex systems. This is a big part of why we play games.

Discuss: How did playing with other people shape the experience?

Because humans are playing Eclipse, the emergent play happens on not only the logical level of angles and vectors but also on social and psychological levels. The first player who decides to break into a run gives permission to other players to start running too—or perhaps inspires someone to stand completely still. The shape of the emergent play is an expression of the group mind of the players.

Discuss: What forms of unexpected play emerged from the game?

The way that Eclipse is played can vary drastically depending on who is playing. Some games become machines for meditative ambling, with everyone walking in lazy circles. Other games become highly athletic contests, with players jockeying for positions and sprinting around the perimeter to find the right angle. Other games find players squeezing together into a tight central cluster.

My most astonishing games of Eclipse have been teaching game designers from a particular (and very large) game company. All of the players formed into a long line—and without saying a word or revealing who they selected, they shuffled back and forth in the line, trying to find the spot that gave everyone an eclipse. I'm not sure if this reflects the bureaucratic impulses of working at a big corporation, a cooperative strain in the local culture, or perhaps game designers using brute-force solution techniques—it's probably some combination of all three! It happened several times independently and completely blew my mind.

Context

The value of playing Eclipse is that all of these ideas are directly and physically embodied as you become a moving cog in a bigger machine. Eclipse is a wonderful introduction to tricky ideas of playing with systems because it is so easy to see how complex behavior emerges from simple rules. It's also a great way to get everyone out of their seats. Eclipse has a storied pedigree: it comes originally from Augusto Boal's *Games for Actors and Non-Actors* (1992) and is also included in *The Infinite Playground* by DeKoven and Gramazio.

ROCK PAPER SCISSORS+

Start with Rock Paper Scissors. Add teams, then invent new symbols, and then turn it into tag. Each new variation offers important lessons about play and design.

1. The basic game

Gather everyone into a big circle. Ask the group for 2 volunteers to step forward and face off for a Rock Paper Scissors match. For clarity, consider reviewing with everyone the 3 classic gestures of the game and the crucial *what beats what*.

Before they play, establish the all-important timing rule: Do the players present their gesture on 1, 2, 3!—or—on 1, 2, 3–shoot! (or something else)? Have the pair of bold volunteers play a match. Let them continue: make it the best 2 out of 3. Then pause for a quick chat about what just happened.

Discuss: Is Rock Paper Scissors a "good game"?

What does everyone think about the game? Is it fun? Is it completely random? Or does it involve some kind of strategy? You may get strong and diverse opinions. It's perfectly OK if some feel that Rock Paper Scissors is a horrible game.

Discuss: Is Rock Paper Scissors a "design"?

There's no doubt that Rock Paper Scissors is a folk game without a particular inventor. In fact, for most of human history, virtually all games were folk games. (Perhaps the most significant event in the history of games is their shift from folk culture to authored media, mostly starting in the late nineteenth century.) Just because no single person conceived Rock Paper Scissors doesn't mean we can't talk about it as a design. It has parts that fit together to make a whole. It has rules and a winning condition—and rituals and meanings. We can use design as a lens for understanding something, even when that something doesn't have a singular author.

What You Need

- 6 or more players, outdoors or in a large room
- 45 minutes

What You Learn

- ◆ How altering game rules changes the resulting play
- ◆ The many ways that a single core mechanic can be modified
- ◆ Social play as a powerful tool in designing experiences

ROCK PAPER SCISSORS+

2. First mod: Teams

The rest of the exercise is a series of modifications to the base game. To begin, divide everyone into 2 teams of approximately equal numbers. Each team forms a huddle and secretly decides which symbol they want to use—Rock, Paper, or Scissors. Let the teams really take their time to discuss and debate. It could be a while! When they are ready, each team selects a representative and the 2 brave avatars face off.

Play another round or two. Feel free to take suggestions about how to position the pair of combatants for maximum drama. (Having them stand back-to-back is my personal favorite.) Pause for a quick conversation about this new team-based modification.

Discuss: What changed in this new version?

This game—which just a moment ago many thought was random, completely without strategy, and devoid of any fun—suddenly transformed. There was a surprising amount for each team to discuss! You only make one choice each time you play: Do you choose Rock, Paper, or Scissors? By slowing down the process, stretching out this choice and how its outcome is revealed, each round of the game becomes encrusted with more meaning. The way that this mod of the game extended and deepened the game's single decision is an incredibly important lesson about designing moments of meaningful choice for players.

Discuss: In what ways did the social interaction change the game experience?

Being forced to make a decision in collaboration with everyone else on your team increases the shared investment in both the choice you make and its result. With every turn, there is more information to take into account. What is the other team planning? Do they think we're going to stick with Paper next round?

Discuss: How did the theatrical ritual of the game contribute to its enjoyment?

By having a representative face off from each group, a new narrative layer is added to the game. Everyone is invested in the spectacle of the contest and its outcome, which gains new dramatic meaning. You can often judge the engagement of a game by the emotional reactions of players. Did this variation result in any outbursts—perhaps some sudden gasps or celebratory cheers?

3. Second mod: Panther Person Porcupine

Announce that something different will change about the game: the 3 symbols. Rock, Paper, and Scissors will become Panther, Person, and Porcupine. Explain how they interact with each other:

- Panther beats Person
  because panthers are terrifying beasts that eat humans

- Person beats Porcupine
  as long as you are wearing sensible footwear

- Porcupine beats Panther
  it's all about the panther's soft belly getting quilled

But how do we signify these new symbols? The group must come up with a gesture—and a sound—for each of the 3 options. Ask for ideas. Try them out. Get goofy. Once you have decided, have the entire group practice Panther Person Porcupine together.

Divide back into the same 2 teams and have each team secretly pick their symbol. Then instead of just 2 players, have everyone line up in 2 long rows facing each other. On your count, everyone reveals their team's chosen symbol and a team will win (or maybe it will be a tie). Try this once or twice. It should be good fun.

Think about: How to get silly

Being loose and unselfconscious in our bodies is an important skill. Creativity, in part, is about feeling free to try things out, so your job is to move participants past any self-conscious rigidity. Lead by silly example. Even more important, help others lead too—letting others demonstrate ideas for funny gestures and sounds gives everyone permission to loosen up and relax.

4. Third mod: Tag

Move straight on to the final variation. You'll keep using the Panther Person Porcupine gestures and add some new rules—to turn Rock Paper Scissors into team-based Panther Person Porcupine Tag.

If you are playing outside, clear the area of any sticks or rocks. Let everyone know that the next game is going to be a bit more physical—this introduces a few new considerations. It's perfectly OK if people want to sit out and watch. Or you might consider adjusting the game to accommodate everyone.

Boundaries: Establish a safe zone on either end of the play area—a tree or other landmark you need to move past in order to be safe. The total play area might be 20 or 30 feet across.

Selection: Each team huddles and secretly selects Panther, Person, or Porcupine as before. Then everyone lines up in the center of the playfield, nose to nose, with each team's safe zone directly behind them. On the count, everyone simultaneously shows their team's chosen symbol.

Resolution: If your team's symbol loses to the other team's symbol, turn around and run to your team's safe zone. If, on the other hand, your team's symbol wins, try to tag as many people on the other team as you can before they reach their safe zone. If it's a tie (both teams selected the same symbol), then hug it out with a nearby opponent from the other team.

Captures: Anyone who is tagged before they reach their safe zone joins the other team. You can keep playing until one team captures everyone else on the other team and wins—although it could take a while! Or play enough rounds so that there is at least one dramatic reversal of fortune. Then gather for a final discussion.

Think about: It's OK to watch

Playing is always voluntary. Respecting physical and social differences means that participation is never mandatory. Bernie DeKoven believed so strongly in the power of not playing that he would sometimes have everyone practice *not* playing a game together.

Think about: Changing the game

If some in your group are put off by the rough-and-tumble of running and chasing (for example, if you are playing on a hard surface), make it a group design challenge to adjust the game and make it safer and more inclusive. What if you can only move in slow motion, or you can only run with both of your knees touching at all times? Games are better when everyone can play.

Think about: Special roles for spectators

Having players watch instead of playing is an excellent option. In sports, we know that cheering spectators help keep the energy of a game going. You can deputize those on the sidelines to help count off each round or serve as referees to watch the safe zones. When it comes time to discuss the game, ask spectators for their opinion first—they have fresh "outside eyes" on the game and may have noticed things that the players did not.

PHYSICAL PLAY

ROCK PAPER SCISSORS+

Discuss: What gives the tag variation its chaotic energy?

Misunderstanding can lead to play. Part of what gives Rock Paper Scissors Tag its wild excitement is the moment of confusion when both teams reveal their symbols. In design we often strive for maximum clarity, but here the false starts and crossed signals are what help fuel the hilarity.

Discuss: How did it feel to change teams?

What was the team psychology of the game? What happened when you were captured by the opposing group? Did you still have some loyalty to your old squad? Or did you turn traitor and reveal your previous team's strategy to your new comrades? Shifting identities and relationships can make for a rich social experience.

Discuss: What emergent narratives came out of the play?

The design of the Tag variation—where "losing" means joining the "winning" team—creates unexpected story moments, like the small band of rag-tag rebels facing off against the massed horde. This shapes the drama of the game in wonderful ways.

Discuss: What stayed consistent across all of the Rock Paper Scissors variations?

None of the mods actually changed the core logic of the game. The first made it a group activity, the second reskinned it with new gestures, and the third added a way to capture members of the other team. The heart of the rules remained consistent, but the game experience changed radically every time. Small changes in social interaction, content, and ritual can be levers for powerful effects.

Discuss: What kinds of creative play emerged in any of the variations?

As always, celebrate moments when players find new ways to inhabit the system of the game. In one of my favorite matches of Rock Paper Scissors Tag, a much smaller team tried the strategy of running away immediately—no matter what symbols were played! When the other team chased them—and it turned out that the smaller team had actually won the face-off—we decided that any tags meant that the tagging player from the bigger team had been captured. Well played!

For remote play

1. **The Basic Game** demonstration works just fine with 2 volunteers.

2. **First mod: Teams** can utilize breakout rooms or separate group chats where each team can confer before reconvening.

3. **Second mod: Panther, Person, Porcupine** also works well online. Alternately, instead of using a Panther, Person, and Porcupine, have the groups redesign the standard Rock Paper Scissors gestures—and add sounds—specifically to work with remote video cameras.

4. **Third mod: Tag** does not translate to remote video. Instead, have the group design a version of the game that everyone can (somehow!) play at the same time. What affordances of the remote platform can be utilized: Text chat for typing in moves? Counting everyone's Rock, Paper, and Scissors gestures as some kind of vote? Turning off your video when you are eliminated? Try out something simple and then iterate with new ideas from the group.

Context

This exercise is a great way to kick off a class or workshop—it gets everyone on their feet for physical play, and it presents wonderful opportunities for discussion and analysis. Rock Paper Scissors Tag (and other Rock Paper Scissors variations) can be found in *The New Games Book* (1976) and its sequel *More New Games* (1981). Both are fantastic sourcebooks for group play activities from Andrew Flugelman and the New Games Foundation, a pioneering organization that helped shape contemporary ideas about play and games.

Stand in a circle.
When it's your turn,
try to tag the hand
of another ninja.
A playground game of
slow-motion battle
and systemic narrative
representation.

NINJA

What You Need

- 5 or more players, in a large room or outdoors
- 30 minutes

What You Learn

- ◆ The way procedures can depict narrative content
- ◆ How physical play can tell dynamic interactive stories
- ◆ Appreciating the invisible details of a game design

1. Teach the game

Ninja requires plenty of space, a circle 10 or 20 feet in diameter. It is best played outside or in a large indoor space. Making a spectacle and getting in the way of passersby can be part of the fun.

Ninja is a slow-motion game—it's safer and more casual than it may seem at first. That said, let everyone know that playing is voluntary. It's totally fine to stand aside and watch. Of course, everyone who wants to join is encouraged to play. Perhaps some players want to watch the first game and then join in next time.

Think about: Inclusive physical play

Whenever you are organizing a physical activity, be open to changing things so that everyone feels comfortable joining. This means being aware of the space where it's taking place, the rules of the game itself (which can always be modified), and even the way that you explain how to play. If someone just wants to watch, that's always an excellent option. Spectators can be referees and help run the game. During the discussion, ask them to comment from their valuable point of view outside the chaos of play. Never stigmatize the decision not to play or the need to play differently.

Ninja works just fine with up to 20 players. More than that and you may want to break into 2 or more groups. That will also speed things up so that you can play more games in the same amount of time.

For help with the rules, on the next page is a set of instructions by designers Sam Farmer, Mihir Sheth, and Asher Volmer. It includes "The Ninja Code," a wonderful articulation of the spirit of how the game is played. I play the most basic version of Ninja—more complex variations can be found online.

Have everyone stand in a big circle and explain how to play. Here is how I like to teach the game:

Look around the circle and take note of who is on your left and your right. Once the game starts, we will take turns around the circle clockwise in this order. Even if you move around and end up in a new location, you will still take your turn in the sequence of the original circle.

To start a game, I will call out "3, 2, 1, NINJA!" And everyone will strike a ninja pose. Let's practice that part now: "3, 2, 1, NINJA!" To play, one person starts, and then everyone takes turns going around the circle. When your turn comes, make one "attack." To attack, you can take one step, or jump with both feet (or even roll on the ground), and then you have to lunge forward and make an attack. A successful attack is when your hand touches the hand of another player. When you make hand-to-hand contact, that person is knocked out of the game. (Ask for 2 players to demonstrate.)

If you are attacked by someone else, you can dodge by moving your body and your arms—but not your feet! You can twist your torso or squat down or move your hands away, but you can't take any kind of step. (Another demonstration of dodging an attack would be useful here.)

When you make an attack or when you dodge, you must freeze after you move. You will end up frozen in your attack or dodge position with your arms outstretched. An attack has to be an assertive gesture—you can't attack but then end up with your arms crossed or your hands in your armpits. You need to really try to get someone and keep your hands out wherever they end up.

The Rules

1. Players form a circle, each standing at arm's length away from each other.

2. On the count of "3, 2, 1, NINJA!" all players jump into ninja poses. Choose your pose wisely!

3. Randomly choose a ninja to begin.

4. On their turn, each player is allowed to make one swift ninja attack. KAPOW! This can involve your whole body. HAYA! Eliminate others by striking their hand—the wrist is not included. You must stiffly hold the position you end your move in.

5. The next player is allowed to move once you have finished your attack.

6. If you are attacked by another player, you may dodge using only your arms.

7. When only 2 players remain, they begin the final duel. The final 2 ninjas stop fighting, bow, and stand back-to-back. On the count of "3, 2, 1, NINJA!" they jump into poses. The ninja with the boldest pose goes first and play resumes normally. The game ends when only one ninja remains.

The Ninja Code

Be ridiculous
The "winner" is not necessarily the most celebrated player; playing with style is more important.

No pullbacks
You must remain in the position you finished your move in.

Fight with honor
If your hand was struck, you're out!

The only referee is the crowd
Impress the crowd and they'll take your side in disputes.

Have fun
There will always be another game of Ninja!

NINJA

2. Play Ninja!

Start playing. Go slowly at first, calling out names to let people know whose turn is next. Note that players do *not* need to attack the next person in the circle; they can move anywhere, attacking backward or leaping across the circle for a surprise attack. Some people will be knocked out before they even have a chance to take a turn—that's OK! The first game is just a learning game.

When there are only 2 people left, move on to the finale, and explain it this way:

> When there are just 2 players remaining, it's time for a final showdown. The 2 survivors walk to the center and stand back-to-back. On the count of 1, 2, 3, NINJA! both of you jump and spin around to face each other. The boldest player goes first (whoever makes the first move), and you alternate turns from there, attacking and dodging until someone is tagged out and only the winner remains.

After the game, applaud the winner. If possible, play a second time—it should go much more smoothly. Anyone who spectated the first game may want to join in the second time.

3. Discuss

Designing new kinds of interactive stories means questioning what we think the very concept of narrative might be. The "story" of Ninja doesn't result from visual effects, character dialog, or a written backstory—it unfolds out of the play itself. Ninja offers many unexpected lessons about how a dynamic system of narrative representation can function to provide a meaningful experience.

Discuss: How is the world of the game established?

In other words, what embedded or intrinsic aspects of Ninja let players know what the game is about? There aren't many—the name is Ninja, of course, and we say things like "3, 2, 1, NINJA!" and "final showdown." That's about it! But these few elements frame the abstract gameplay in a very effective way, recasting the entire experience through the lens of a dangerous—if cartoony—ninja battle. The title Ninja is a kind of cognitive frame players step through that helps give meaning to everything else.

Discuss: How does the theme of the game emerge from the play?

There are other aspects of ninja-ness to Ninja that are not explicitly defined in advance but appear during the game. As players strike ninja poses, the entire circle resembles a freeze frame from a martial arts movie. Moving between your frozen opponents with lightning speed makes you feel like an action hero. These emergent aspects of the representation (the improvised gestures and action-movie tableau) spring out of the dynamics of play.

Discuss: Dig deeper. What specific details of the design build the game's depiction?

The rule that you need to tag another player's hand with your hand and then freeze shapes the very particular gestures that players' bodies take. If this rule were changed—if you could tag a player anywhere—the gameplay might be more flexible but the play would lose its very Ninja-like spectacle. This is design in action: very particular design choices resulting in very particular experiences.

Discuss: Beyond the core interaction, what shapes the arc of play?

Besides one-on-one attacks, the design of Ninja also creates larger arcs of experience. As more players are knocked out, the game gets riskier, with nearby opponents moving more frequently. The pace steadily accelerates, climaxing in a final duel that provides a satisfying showdown conclusion.

Context

Play combat has a long history, dating back to the venerable Society for Creative Anachronism (1966) and more recent LARP (Live Action Role-Playing) culture. Ninja is a folk game that emerged out of comic/anime/game cons and now has a wide international following. It is not only a blast to play but embodies many nuanced ideas about systems of procedural representation. Ninja is passed from player to player—I was lucky enough to learn it from designers Sam Farmer, Mihir Sheth, and Asher Volmer, who first showed me how to play at the IndieCade Festival of Independent Games many years ago.

THE LANGUAGE GAME

Two volunteers alternate saying random words. By gradually adding constraints, the activity evolves into a real game. A lesson in play and meaning.

THE LANGUAGE GAME

1. Name any word

Ask for 2 volunteers—they don't even need to get up out of their seats. Then tell them how to play. My explanation usually goes something like this:

> We're going to play a game, and I'm going to explain how it works, step-by-step. We might not get it completely right the first time around, so thanks for your patience! Here's how it works. Each of the 2 players is going to alternate saying a single word. The only rule is that you can't repeat a word that has been said before by either player. Are you ready? Let's try.

Starting with one of the players, have them alternate speaking words. Likely, their words will be somewhat random—they might hit upon a topic or pattern, or they might not. After they bounce words back and forth a few times, you can pause the game.

What You Need

- 2 players (works as a demonstration for a bigger group)
- 15 minutes

What You Learn

- Cleverly limiting interaction is the key to meaningful play
- Play happens when there is a balance of freedom and constraint
- Language is a space of meaning where we can play

2. Limit the domain

The next step is to restrict the content of the words they can select. Look for some theme or idea in what they have said so far: if they named an animal, make the domain animals. If they used someone's name as a word, make it names. Don't make the domain too narrow (like restricting it to just colors)—they will need a lot of words to be able to choose from. My go-to category is food—here's what I would say to introduce that topic as the constraint:

> OK, that was a good start, but not yet really a fun game. Let's add a rule and see what happens. We are going to keep all of the rules we had— the players are going to alternate saying single words, and a word can't be repeated. Now we are going to add one more rule. One of you mentioned coffee—so let's make food and beverages the new rule. You can only say words that are things to eat and drink—fruits, vegetables, dishes, drinks. Ready? Let's go.

Then they can play with these new rules, with the 2 players alternating stating a word within the theme. They can stop after they say a few words each.

3. First and last letters

Likely, the game was less exciting that time around because there were fewer opportunities for strange and unexpected words. You're still not there yet—it's time for a final variation. You can introduce it like this:

> Well, well, well. I think that last rule actually made the game less interesting than before. But that's not the players' fault—that's on me! It's my responsibility as the designer to make this game better. So let's try one more rule change and see what happens.
> We're going to keep all of the rules we had so far: the players are going to alternate saying a word, and a word can't be repeated. You can only say words that are food and beverages [or whatever content constraint you chose]. And here's the new rule: after the first word is spoken, the *last letter* of that word needs to be the *first letter* of the next word. And the last letter of that word will be the first letter of the next word, and so on. Ready? Let's try.

This time, things should feel different. What had been a rote set of chores has suddenly evolved into a challenging game. You are likely to get some tense moments with the appearance of particularly difficult letters; unexpected patterns (like a run of plurals that all end with s); spectators shouting help from the sidelines; or even some creative rule-breaking, such as using 2 words ("decaf coffee" as a d word).

Allow them to play several words each. End with applause, and thank the volunteer players.

PLAY WITH MEANING

4. Discuss

What just happened? Draw everyone's attention to the difference between the 3 versions of the game and the transformation of the experience when the final version occurred.

Discuss: What changed in the final version of the game?

As soon as the third variation started, there should have been a noticeable shift in the energy of the room as everyone in the audience leaned forward and began thinking of words to say. Suddenly, the 2 players felt pressure to perform. Point out new kinds of creative play that happened in the third version. What exactly caused the change?

Discuss: How do constraints build meaningful interaction?

Constraints construct play. We often think that games are about limitless power—traveling to fantastic worlds, being anyone, having amazing super abilities—and, perhaps, they sometimes feel that way to players. However, from a designer's point of view, constraints help build the experience of a game. Each version of the exercise added more constraints, and more constraints made the game better.

Discuss: What are some examples of constraints in games?

Constraints are a part of every game. If you are playing a board game with a pair of dice, there are so many things you could do with the dice—juggle them, make them into earrings, grind them into powder—but you don't do any of those things. You do only one very particular thing. When it is your turn, you roll the dice, count the dots on the faceup sides, and move your piece on the board exactly that number of spaces. Games are built from these kinds of constraints.

Discuss: Are more constraints always better?

Definitely not! You could add another rule to the Language Game exercise—perhaps, words must be exactly 6 letters long—but that would make it too difficult to play. Game rules need to create a space for play that is not too loose and not too restricted. Like a planet that can support life, it's hard to find just the right balance of constraints and freedom that can result in a rich ecosystem of creative play.

Discuss: What is the relationship between creativity and constraint?

Good design can encourage creative play. It's a paradox that play emerges out of the limitations of constraints. In games, creative play is possible only when there are enough constraints to productively structure the behavior of players. Like a musician who learns over time how to groove with their instrument, you become a virtuoso of a system by exploring its possibilities and cleverly figuring out how to make it do something unexpected and new.

Context

The core of this exercise is a folk game sometimes called Geography, which traditionally uses the names of cities, states, and countries as the content constraint. (It was a favorite travel game in my family when I was growing up.) The Language Game exercise packs a lot of incredibly important ideas into a very small package—it has clear lessons about designing with constraints that are applicable to all kinds of interactive experiences.

SURREAL -IST GAMES

Three ways to play with language and images, including two versions of the famous Exquisite Corpse. These creative exercises foster a collaborative state of mind.

SURREALIST GAMES

1. Questions and Answers

To prepare for this first of the three games, you will need the group to generate some Questions and Answers. If you have a lot of participants (more than a dozen), half of them can write one Question and the other half can write one Answer. For smaller groups, each person can write one or more of each type. They will write each Question or Answer on a separate index card.

Questions take the definitional form of:

"What is _____?"

What is love?

What is the most horrible thing that has ever happened to you?

What is in my pocket?

What You Need

- 3 or more players, in person or remotely online
- 45 minutes
- Index cards, paper, and writing/drawing utensils

What You Learn

- How creativity emerges from constraint-based interaction
- Models for designing collaborative storytelling
- How to design for audience-generated content

A black void from which nothing can escape

That feeling when a word is on the tip of your tongue

Tuesday

Answers should be possible responses to a "What is _____ ?" question.

Gather up the cards, being sure to keep Questions and Answers in 2 separate facedown piles. To play, draw a random Question and read it out loud—and then draw and read a random Answer to that Question. There should be a surprisingly high number of fantastic Question-and-Answer matches.

Discuss: What about the details of the design makes the exercise work?

Questions and Answers relies on productive constraints. The game works so well in part because the writing is funneled into a modular structure in which every answer can potentially fit every question. Imagine a version where questions and answers do not follow the "What is _____ ?" structure but could take any form. They just wouldn't flow together in the same way. When designing interactive activities, it all comes down to the details.

Discuss: Beyond individual cards, how does the whole collection make meaning?

The pairs of questions and answers gain additional meaning when there are lots of them to compare with each other. Some pairings feel incredibly logical. Others are wildly surreal. This mix actually helps accentuate both ends of the spectrum. When we read them all together, there is a heightened appreciation for not only serendipitous sensemaking but also for bizarre juxtapositions.

Discuss: How does the ritual of the exercise contribute to its experience?

The enjoyment of the game is aided by the drama of presentation. Pleasure and surprise are enhanced because the group produced the cards themselves. As the cards are read one by one, you wait to see if yours will come up and how it will be paired. The reveal of each new card feels like getting a new and exciting present. Will the game be better or worse if you play again with the same set of cards?

PLAY WITH MEANING

SURREALIST GAMES

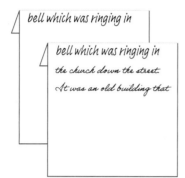

2. Exquisite Corpse (with words)

The classic Exquisite Corpse game is about making a random statement together, piece by piece. In this exercise, you will play a second Surrealist game, with written language.

Everyone takes a piece of paper and composes the beginning of a story, writing exactly 2 lines of text at the top of the paper. (It's OK—and maybe even preferred—if you end midsentence.) Then the paper is folded back so that only the second line is visible. After that, hand the folded paper to the person on your left.

Take the paper you just received and write 2 new lines, continuing the story forward from the single line that is visible. Fold the paper back again so that only your last line is visible. Pass the paper to the left again, and continue the story by writing 2 more lines. Fold the paper over again in the same way. Then pass to the fourth person in the chain, who will finish the story with a final pair of lines that brings it to some kind of conclusion. Have everyone read their stories to the group.

Discuss: Does Exquisite Corpse put you in a different state of mind?

Inspired by nonlinear dreams and the creativity of children, surrealists believed that playing games like Exquisite Corpse could bring about new states of consciousness. What is the difference between writing a story normally and writing through a collective process? How does collaborative authorship affect the experience of writing and our relationship with the final result?

Discuss: How could you use this generative structure in a different way?

The basic Exquisite Corpse structure has been used to fuel many projects, such as *The Narrative Corpse* (1995), a chain story by 69 comic artists, edited by Art Spiegelman. I have even used Exquisite Corpse as a way to generate a set of semirandom game rules (which are full of holes and contradictions that need to be fixed). It's a versatile model that can be extended to many kinds of collaborations.

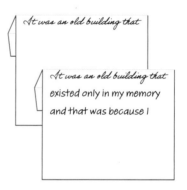

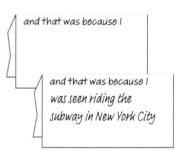

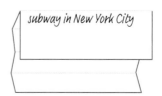

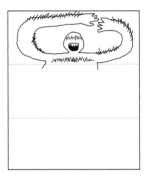

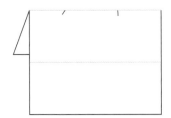

3. Exquisite Corpse (with images)

The final game is the drawing-based version of Exquisite Corpse. Everyone takes a piece of letter-size paper and starts by folding it into 3 equal sections (like you are putting it into an envelope). Begin by drawing in the top third of the paper, staying within the section but letting just a few lines pass over the fold into the middle section.

When everyone is done, they fold the paper backward so that their drawing is hidden, except for the few lines that are poking into the middle third of the paper. Pass the paper to the person on your left. Then everyone takes the paper they were just handed and uses the lines as a starting point to draw in the middle section, again letting a few lines stray down just over the fold into the bottom.

The paper is folded backward again to hide the previous drawings and passed to the left. Taking the paper you were handed, everyone fills the bottom portion of the paper, continuing from the lines that were drawn over the fold. When they are finished, reveal all of the drawings and pin them up or place them on a table side by side.

Discuss: What are the constraints that make the game work?

Making a drawing from scratch on a blank piece of paper is an intimidating prospect for most of us. The structured interaction of Exquisite Corpse—from the paper folded in thirds to the guidelines left over the fold—gently facilitates the experience. These designed constraints allow a sense of comfort that enables creativity to emerge.

Discuss: How does the structure of the exercise encourage collaboration?

The shared authorship of each drawing also gives permission to be less precious about what each individual contributes. In Exquisite Corpse, we are collaborating, but not in ways that we understand in the moment we are doing it. The surprise of the final reveal is part of the experience too—a satisfying moment you share with your co-creators.

Discuss: What are some general lessons for creativity or collaboration?

The secret to creativity is often about limiting what you do. Designing within a tight schedule, or for a particular audience, or with concrete creative goals in mind, helps focus the process. Identifying those constraints can help a group find their vibe together. When it comes to designing creative activities for an audience, limiting what they do paradoxically frees up inhibitions, and they usually end up in more unexpected and interesting places.

Context

Surrealists played these and many other games in the early twentieth century, but their origin can be traced back to traditional folk games. More examples of playful ways to get in touch with your nonrational mind—from Automatic Writing to media-jamming Détournement—can be found in *A Book of Surrealist Games* (1995) by Alastair Gotchie and Mel Gooding. Surrealist games can open up ideas of narrative, collaboration, and shared authorship. They are great examples of tight interaction design that produces wildly unpredictable results.

SYSTEMS

A system isn't just any old collection of things. A system is an interconnected set of elements that is coherently organized in a way that achieves something. If you look at that definition closely for a minute, you can see that a system must consist of three kinds of things: elements, interconnections, and a function or purpose.

For example, the elements of your digestive system include teeth, enzymes, stomach, and intestines. They are interrelated through the physical flow of food, and through an elegant set of regulating chemical signals. The function of this system is to break down food into its basic nutrients and to transfer those nutrients into the bloodstream (another system) while discarding unusable wastes.

A football team is a system with elements such as players, coach, field, and ball. Its interconnections are the rules of the game, the coach's strategy, the players' communications, and the laws of physics that govern the motions of ball and players. The purpose of the team is to win games, or have fun, or get exercise, or make millions of dollars, or all of the above.

A school is a system. So is a city, and a factory, and a corporation, and a national economy. An animal is a system. A tree is a system, and a forest is a larger system that encompasses subsystems of trees and animals. The earth is a system. So is the solar system; so is a galaxy. Systems can be embedded in systems, which are embedded in yet other systems.

Is there anything that is not a system? Yes—a conglomeration without any particular interconnections or function. Sand scattered on a road by happenstance is not, itself, a system. You can add sand or take away sand and you still have just sand on the road. Arbitrarily add or take away football players, or pieces of your digestive system, and you quickly no longer have the same system.

Donella H. Meadows
Thinking in Systems

A FEW WAYS TO THINK ABOUT SYSTEMS

CONNECTING INTERCONNECTIONS

Systems are everywhere. Thinking in terms of systems illuminates how parts become wholes and how we relate to the world and to each other.

A system is a set of parts that interrelate to form a whole. Just about anything can be a system: bees in a hive, characters in a story, pieces on a game board. Sharpening your ability to think in terms of systems is part of being literate today.

Why? We are living in a world increasingly defined by systems: systems of communication, commerce, transportation, information. Becoming fluent in systems thinking is exactly like the proverbial fish becoming aware of its surrounding water.

There's no secret to systems thinking—you just need to cultivate an interest in how things are put together. Examples are everywhere. In New York City, where I live, I have always been struck by the rhythm of the traffic signals. There is a particularly generous amount of time between the moment when pedestrians see "don't walk" and when cross-traffic cars get a green light and move across their path. In other words, for several seconds after you are told not to walk, it is in fact still quite safe to do so. This has led to a kind of vicious cycle: New Yorkers, who are always in a hurry anyway, have learned to ignore the "don't walk" signs. As a result, street crossings are dominated by pushy pedestrians who battle with impatiently honking cars for the right of way.

When I visit Boston, on the other hand, I quickly need to adjust my sense of pedestrian entitlement. There is a much smaller timing buffer zone: when the crosswalk signal blinks a steady "don't walk," you can count on cars immediately speeding straight toward you across the intersection. I find that there is a much more respectful deference shown by drivers (who will politely stop to let people cross) and pedestrians (who don't jump in front of oncoming cars to hurry across a street). It's a completely different set of sensibilities.

What is the cause and effect here? Is the design of traffic-light timing responsible for the nuances of a particular city's street-crossing culture? Or are they a reflection of preexisting, local notions of proper traffic etiquette? How does the traffic-light system connect with other systems, such as the economic systems that determine who can afford to be traveling in a car in a particular neighborhood? How do all of these systems evolve and change? (By the time you are reading this, I'm sure that NYC's signal timing has already been redesigned.)

If these kinds of questions start to tickle your curiosity, congratulations. You are experiencing the detective thrill of analyzing, critiquing, and perhaps even redesigning systems.

An investigation of a system often begins with mechanical details—electronic timers, crosswalk sensors, "don't walk" signals. But it is never enough to just look at the isolated elements. The importance of systems comes from the whole that emerges from the parts: How utterances become a conversation. How organisms become an ecosystem. How individuals become a community. For a designer, systems always connect back to people—to emotion, psychology, and culture. To the water in which we swim every day, that connects everything to everything else.

DYNAMIC BEHAVIORS

More important than the isolated parts of a system is how it behaves over time. Snowball and catch-up effects are powerful tools for shaping what systems do.

Complicated systems are never just a static formation, like the legs of a stool holding up a seat. A complex system is more like a machine with intricate moving parts or an organism responding to constant input. The relationships between elements change dynamically over time.

Let's say you're playing a game of Chess. Your opponent makes a burst of strong moves, capturing some of your key pieces. A snowball effect starts to happen—the fact that your opponent has more pieces on the board means they can press their advantage, leading to yet more captures and even more dominance. Your opponent's advantage accelerates, building on itself in an increasingly inevitable, vicious-cycle feedback loop.

The same reinforcing cycle happens in real-time strategy games, when doing well early on helps you win even faster. And it happens in real-world economics, as the rich use personal wealth to avoid paying taxes and get even richer. An ability to gather and deploy resources lets you gather and deploy even more resources: a small advantage quickly becomes a huge power disparity. In the United States, politicians in power often get to redraw their own state voting districts. The result? The snowballing phenomenon of gerrymandering. Those in power can entrench their position, ensuring that they stay in power and entrench even more. These kinds of accelerating processes, also called *positive* or *reinforcing* feedback loops, aren't always bad. A snowballing process can help push a game toward conclusion and keep it from stalling out in a grueling stalemate. In contrast, reinforcing loops in law and policy can too often reinforce inequality. (Indeed, democracy is a system too, with its own dynamic behaviors—a system very much in desperate need of redesign.)

Sometimes the opposite of a snowball occurs: catch-up mechanics. When you are behind in many racing games, your virtual car is given a "rubber-banding" boost so that it springs forward and doesn't fall too far behind the lead car. Why? Because closer matches, in which vehicles are jockeying tightly for position, are exciting! Unlike snowball effects that magnify differences, catch-up mechanics assist those who are behind (or drag back those who are ahead), helping to keep everyone's hope for victory alive and to maintain uncertainty until the end of the game. Similar catch-up dynamics, also known as *negative* or *balancing* feedback loops, regulate heating and cooling of buildings, or happen when an overzealous predator reduces its own food supply, or when customers complain and by doing so improve corporate policies and reduce complaints.

The classic Eight-Ball version of Pool (circa 1900) has both species of system behaviors built into the design—something I learned from game design educator Jesse Fuchs. When you sink one of your balls, there is a snowball feedback loop: you immediately get to take another shot, rewarding your success and compounding your progress toward victory. Yet there is simultaneously a catch-up mechanic at work too: the more balls you sink, the fewer targets there are on the table, and the harder it is for you to find a clear shot, which helps players who are behind. The dramatic pacing of Pool emerges through this interplay between snowball mechanics that add momentum and catch-up mechanics that level the playing field.

Snowball and catch-up loops are incredibly influential in sculpting the dynamic pace and balance of a system. Is your designed experience dragging on and lacking dramatic tension? Is it diminishing or exaggerating inequalities? Uncovering hidden feedback loops is a powerful tool for critiquing and redesigning relationships of power—both in and out of games.

ARTIFICIAL LANGUAGES

Designers invent systems of meaning that are built out of relationships. The meanings of these systems are both separate from but also very much a part of the rest of culture.

Games are systems in many ways: they are narrative systems, mathematical systems, social systems. They can also be thought of as systems of signification. In other words, games give meaning to things. They add an extra layer of significance to human activity.

Squeezing your fingers into a fist can mean a lot of things. It might mean "Go defense!" as you cheer on your favorite team from the stands. Or maybe you are balling up your hand in genuine anger. Or playfully winding up a Popeye-style air punch. On the other hand, if you are playing Rock Paper Scissors, a fist means something incredibly specific. It signifies an object: a rock.

And that's not all. This rock has its own special meaning—it exists within a miniature universe of relationships. Rock beats Scissors, which beats Paper. And Paper beats Rock. The game of Rock Paper Scissors gives these gestures interrelated meaning.

As in a dictionary, meaning is about relationships. Looking up one definition—the meaning of a word—leads you to look up others, and still others. A game is a web of interconnected meanings, all supporting and referencing each

other. When players agree to play a game, they agree to accept and abide by these meanings and to explore how they might play out when they set them in motion. A designer is like the inventor of a new language. As you make a game, or any kind of system, you assign meanings— to the participants, spaces, objects, and actions. Players employ these elements of meaning in the dialog of play.

In part these languages are artificial—they invent meanings separate from the usual state of affairs. In *Homo Ludens* (1938), historian Johan Huizinga famously called games a "magic circle," a sacred place defined by its separateness in time and space from ordinary life. For instance, if you and I play a game of Chess, a whole lattice of special signification springs up. Time and space and identity gain new layers. Is it my turn or your turn? Is the Rook on this square or that square? Is my black King in danger? It's only when a game is being played that any of these questions matter, or even make sense, to anyone.

In some ways, games are separated from life outside the game. At the very same time, games are, of course, always already a part of real-world lives and politics and economies. Displaying a Chess set in my apartment traffics with meanings outside of any individual game. Is it an antique Chess set that conspicuously conveys wealth and intellectual depth? Or a Simpsons Chess set that broadcasts ironic pop-culture savvy? Any game is part of larger local and global media cultures. Games are part of capitalist business practices. Games perpetuate racist, sexist, ableist, and other stereotypes. Is the fact that the Queen is the most powerful piece an instance of stealth feminism— or is it all ultimately in service of the master King?

As a designer, you are concocting and remixing these languages—in part inventing artificial meanings and in part building on cultural meanings that already exist. Your newly invented structures gain their meaning from what came before. For example, you redesign Rock Paper Scissors into Protestor Police Attorney. So... what beats what?

ACTIONS AND OUTCOMES

Interactive systems connect choices to results. These choices gain meaning as they are integrated with each other and the outcomes of the choices are communicated by the system.

What does it mean to interact with something? You try something out—press a button, or open a door, or ask a question—and then something happens. You take an action, and there is some kind of result. Even if the outcome is that nothing happens at all.

Action leads to outcome. When you design an interactive system, part of what you are doing is connecting events to results. You are defining how the system will work—what exactly will happen when somebody does something. These are the atoms by which interactive meaning is made.

When you spell a word in Scrabble and score a dozen points, you are not just taking part in cold numerical logic. You are enacting a moment of *meaning*. You are giving significance to the action of placing letter tiles on the board. This meaning is bound up with other meanings. For example, was it an unusual word that shows how clever you are? Did your move open up opportunities on the board for other players? Or perhaps block them from a triple-word score? Are you winning the game now? And do you really care about winning anyway? The design of Scrabble gives this web of actions and effects significance. Design is a process of building a context where human activity—like arranging tiles on a table—gains meaning.

One layer of action-outcome design has to do with the actual logical result of a choice— the way that choices and outcomes are *integrated* into the warp and weft of other choices. If the points you earned for playing a Scrabble word were completely randomized, then it wouldn't matter what you did. That's a problem: if the choice really doesn't matter, then the action is literally meaningless. As players explore your design, they have faith that the actions they take will add up to something—a gripping story, a risky strategy, a fun way to get through the current level. Integrating actions and outcomes is how that happens.

Another layer of action-outcome design is making the participant aware of what happens. The system needs to make its ever-changing state clear to players. The logical meaning that connects outcome to action has to be *communicated*. Video games go to all kinds of lengths to broadcast what is happening. When you press a button and fire your laser on an *Asteroids* (1979) arcade machine, many things happen all at once: a beam emerges from your spaceship, along with the sharp bleep of a laser blast. The laser beam flies forward, and if it collides with an asteroid, then—ker-blammo! More visual and audio effects depict the results.

Choices add up. They gain meaning by being integrated with other actions and communicated to those in the game. They also gain meaning from the surrounding contexts in which they are made. Why are you playing *Asteroids*? To kill time, to compete in a tournament, to impress a date? What does playing *Asteroids* say about you as a game player? Or as a person?

Living in a world of systems means that we all must take responsibility for the ways our actions have outcomes outside of ourselves. Case in point: the climate crisis. Our dire planetary situation demonstrates how so many human actions add up to dangerously integrated global systemic effects. Meanwhile, on the public side of the crisis, organizations like Extinction Rebellion have taken up the challenge to communicate the need for taking immediate drastic action, through civil disobedience and creative protests. Actions have outcomes— which ones are you going to take?

THE PARADOX OF UNCERTAINTY

Every game needs to keep its conclusion shrouded in mystery while simultaneously reassuring players that their actions will amount to something they can anticipate in advance.

Uncertainty in games is a delicious contradiction. On the one hand, games must surprise us. If we knew how a game would end, we wouldn't ever start in the first place. A game with a wholly predictable ending is a foregone conclusion, without any suspense to keep us guessing to the end. This is what keeps sports fans in their seats—as long as they don't know who is going to win, they are going to stick around until the final buzzer.

On the other hand, the opposite is also true. In the midst of all this uncertainty, players also need some kind of assurance about the efficacy of choices they make. We need to know that choices add up—that each decision has some logical connection to the next—and brings us closer to a desired conclusion. Actions in a game are not just a random series of events: what happened in the past connects to what will happen in the future. Without a sense of progression—the dramatic arc of a story, the unfolding of a clever strategy, the accumulation of clues that solve a mystery—the choices we take are a nonsensical jumble. We need some sense of certainty—a faith in the system—that our actions build on each other to achieve a greater meaning.

This is a delicate and powerful paradox. Game designers need to keep uncertainty alive until the bitter end, even though every step along the way has to exhibit a clarity of action-causing outcomes. It's all a bit weird. Like being led on a journey by a mischievous guide who gives you explicit directions about which way to turn at each intersection—but refuses to say exactly where you are going to end up.

Both parts of this equation offer profound design challenges. You must establish the familiar certainty of meaningful interaction while, at the same time, digging mysteries so deep that they might never be fully exhausted. Or at the very least, somehow keep the fans in their seats until the final buzzer sounds.

SYSTEMIC STORYTELLING

Interactive narratives can leverage traditional storytelling techniques, but their untapped power lies in harnessing the energy of dynamic systems.

We hear a lot about "the power of storytelling"—how stories create impactful experiences that can move hearts, change minds, or get us to purchase product X over Y. Designers telling narratives interactively—with a video game, or in VR, or across a network of smartphones—are often particularly taken with the potential of story. Story often gets discussed like it is some kind of universal elixir that can be magically added to improve an experience. Unfortunately, you can't just paint "story" over a structure and make it better. Meaningful storytelling always engages with the minute particulars of a cultural form—actors on a stage, panels of a comic, the social affordances of online media.

Here's another way of saying the same thing: for me, the question is never, How can a game tell a story that is *as good as* a story in a book, or a play, or a film? Instead I like to ask, What is a story that could *only* be told in a game? In other words, if we made use of the unique characteristics of interactive systems to tell stories, what exactly would we get?

In our book *Rules of Play*, Katie Salen and I use the terms *embedded* and *emergent* to describe the ways games tell stories. Embedded elements are preauthored, fixed narrative components—the names of Ms. Pac-Man and her ghost antagonists, the graphics on the arcade cabinet, the animated opening attract loop. Emergent elements, in contrast, are dynamic procedures that help build the narrative—the AI routines that craft a different personality for each ghost, the difficulty curve that results in an arc of escalating tension, the rule-driven moments of dramatic reversal when a power pill turns the hunted into the hunter (*Ms. Pac-Man*, 1982).

While games can make use of many kinds of embedded content—from musical scores to pre-scripted dialog—the emergent parts of a narrative system, based on the systemic, participatory characteristics of games, are what unlock the unique potentials for games to play with narrative. One of my favorite examples is the children's board game Up the River (1988). Each player moves their little wooden boat pieces along a river that is composed of a row of movable tiles. Every turn, the last river tile physically shifts to the front of the river, which pushes the rest of the river—and all of the players' boats—backward one space. This physical system of cycling tiles is an amazingly expressive way of representing the feeling of swimming upstream. It's so satisfyingly frustrating to see your miniature fleet flowing back against the current. Up the River does have embedded components (the title, the box cover illustration, the shapes of the boat pieces), but the brilliance of how it depicts its world comes from the emergent elements.

Stories will continue to be an important way for humans to find and create meaning. What is a story you could tell *only* through play? More important, what do you want to say by telling it?

STYLIZED SIMULATIONS

Games express their subject matter not just through fixed media but through dynamic processes. Yet every simulation leaves out much more than it includes.

Games are representations. They depict real and fictional worlds, from the mercantile commerce of Renaissance Italy to fantastical lands of marshmallow monsters. They express this content through just about every kind of media: the written word, animated images, musical scores. Games can also provide a different kind of depiction. Something less like prerecorded images and sound and more like a dynamic situation. Games can depict their subject matter through algorithms, procedures, and participatory interaction. In other words, they simulate—they enact representation through process.

The witch character in the video game *The Legend of Zelda: A Link to the Past* (1991) is depicted very much as a stylized cartoon witch. She has a pointed hat and chin, stands next to a bubbling cauldron, and cackles in her speech bubble when she talks. She is also simulated through more procedural means. Her house is hidden in a dangerous forest, and to find her you have to stray from the safer and more "civilized" village—her location on the world map is itself part of her depicted identity. Once you reach her, she offers to turn your mushrooms into magic powder. This is

another procedural characteristic that helps her simulate the character of a witch—a liminal figure that can magically transform nature. The witch's memorable representation in the game combines fixed media characteristics (her appearance and dialog) with more procedurally simulated ones (her hidden location and in-game abilities).

When you are considering how to represent your subject matter in a game, don't just focus on how things will look and sound. Consider also what procedural means you can engage as part of your representation. What sorts of cause and effect, interaction and outcome, can you build into your content? How are you going to simulate your subject matter?

The challenge, of course, is that every simulation is a radical simplification—a stylized, toylike version of its subject. If you are designing a game about gardening, are you going to focus on the sunlight and water that the plants need to grow? The environmental impact of your fertilizer choices? How to win the most beautiful garden contest? Your relationships with neighbors, as you chat with them while working in the garden? You can't include all of these! What you decide to depict depends on what kind of game you want to make.

It's more than window dressing. In establishing causes and effects, a simulation embodies ideologies about how the world works. Why does a bigger garden earn more points? What does your design say about what constitutes success? Or people? Or history?

Any simulation is a statement about the mechanics of reality. Crucially, what you exclude is as important as what you decide to include. Many classic board games are premised on questionable depictions of colonialism—from historical scenarios that whitewash the economics of slavery to fictional worlds that celebrate exploitation of subjugated territory. Often, on the level of abstract gameplay, these games are incredibly well designed, with elegant mechanics and layered strategic challenges. At the same time, on the ethical level of what and how they depict their subject matter, they are egregiously irresponsible.

Every game is a speculation: to stimulate is to envision something that might not exist right now. So be thoughtful about what you represent, and be aware of what you leave out. What kind of world does your world envision?

GOALS WITHIN GOALS

Goals in games—
short-term or long-term,
defined by the designer
or invented by players—
are a powerful way
of keeping us engaged.
Is there any escape
from them?

Every game is a double seduction. First, you need to be convinced to play, to enter into the "magic circle." But for the game to have any life, you also need to keep playing—to imbue the system with effort and keep it moving forward until it reaches a conclusion.

Getting someone to start playing is part of design. What will draw someone's eye to a listing on a search results page or a box on a living-room board game shelf? How do you compel your audience to download and install the app, or take down the box and share it with friends? Once they have ventured inside, the second part of the seduction begins. What keeps them in the game? What will intrigue an audience—for days, weeks, or years? The answers are different for each game. One set of tools that can help keep players engaged with a game, that can structure their curiosity and entangle their desire, are goals.

Part of what defines a game is the goal. An outcome. Winning or losing, or receiving a score. A final goal certainly doesn't have to be part of every kind of play, yet in a very traditional sense, a goal is what makes a game a game. Friends can casually ski down a slope together, or they can race against the clock to see who can get a faster time. Game designer Frank Lantz calls the goal

of a game a kind of gravity. It orders events, letting you know which way is up and which way is down. Without a goal, how do you know that a move was good or bad? How can you decide what you should do next?

In many kinds of play, we invent our own goals. There isn't a final ending to reach in open-play "sandbox" games like *SimCity* (1989). You can decide what kind of city you want to make and the decisions that take you closer to or farther away from that vision. You are free to evolve and adjust your goals as you go. Yet it's even more complicated than that. Goals are not just about the final conclusion. Games are systems of goals within goals. Short-term goals (getting past a tricky double jump) become medium-term goals (collecting enough energy for the next level up) become long-term goals (beating the final boss). All of them interconnect, flowing into and through each other. The double jump lets you reach more energy. Leveling up with that energy gives you abilities to beat the final boss. Interlocking goals become a taut web of enticing possibility that unfolds into a dense landscape of meaning.

Goals are a trail of breadcrumbs, sometimes explicitly designed, sometimes scattered by players themselves. As you plot moment to moment, achieving and planning, strategizing and improvising, goals keep your head in the game. They enwrap our minds in a state of play. Until, of course, we reach the end. There is a poetic tragedy to games and goals, whose delicate birth is always rounded by a driving stampede to their own death. Games desperately beg us to begin, only so that they can play themselves out, reach a conclusion, and exhaust their possibilities in a final outcome.

WILLING SUBMISSION

When players play a game again and again, it can mean they have discovered meaningful play. But when does positive replayability become negative compulsion?

In the game industry, the word *addictive* has traditionally been a positive term. The idea that a player would want to spend time with a game, returning to it again and again, often means success. Addictive in this sense is another word for compelling, engaging, or just plain fun.

Outside of the game industry, of course, addiction means a compulsive obsession. According to the DSM guide (the American Psychiatric Association's *Diagnostic and Statistical Manual of Mental Disorders*), people can get clinically addicted to many things, from exercise to shopping to drugs. In the early decades of video games, there was often a stereotype of games as destructively addictive and violent. There were many attempts to regulate games not as a form of free speech and artistic expression but instead as a harmful vice.

Addiction to games is a complicated topic. Playing with desire is what art and media and entertainment often do—keeping us in suspense, gripping our emotions, thrilling us in the catharsis between tension and release. Games do tease and titillate our craving for feedback, through rewards and punishments, goals and achievements. Game designer Brian Moriarty

has used the term *entrainment* to describe the curious patterned repetition of gameplay. In French, the verb *entrainer* means both "to carry along" and "to trap." It so wonderfully captures the double significance of being pulled into an experience that we willingly enter, just so that we can be pleasantly manipulated. This is part of the beauty and power of games.

For centuries, games have leveraged this power to generate capital, from ancient sheep knucklebone gambling to collectible-card booster packs and quarter-sucking arcade machines. In recent years, though, something has changed: the digital game industry has dialed things up to eleven. Many games desperately squeeze every drop of possible revenue from players, through virtual item collecting, random loot-box drops, or gate fees for the ability to keep playing. Video game publishers employ whole departments of game design quants, whose task is to analyze and instrumentalize player behavior, strategizing how to capture more time and attention, cultivate more profitable player "whales," all to acquire more revenue and profit per user. This is not the case for all games and all designers, but it is a disturbing trend.

Of course, this practice is not limited to games. Digital apps and social media of all kinds are appropriating the surface of games, the levels and points and delicious rewards that compel desire. They stream deceptive advertisements, surreptitiously steal data, hoodwink users into making purchases, and manipulate them by carrying them along and entrapping them.

These dark design patterns are part of the bigger global trend of digital capitalism. That's not to say that games aren't part of the problem—they definitely are! But perhaps they can be a part of the solution as well. How do we avoid doing capitalism's dirty work of designing perpetual dissatisfaction? What other options are there?

Remember that above all, play is voluntary. When we are not willing participants in the dance of desire, we are no longer playing. Truly addicted play—or apps that secretly steal our data or trick us into spending money when we don't want to—are not only playing unfairly, they are not really playing at all. They violate the spirit of play. Your job as a designer is to fight for ethical design every day through the thoughtful things you make—and also, of course, to foster more genuine play in the world.

AGAINST GAMIFICATION

Don't believe the hype: gamification extracts the surface of games without appreciating their depths. In doing so, it cheapens both play and players.

In recent years, the idea that games can be a useful way of designing other things—that we can gamify a classroom, a corporate division, or a smartphone app—has become all the rage. Rage is right: when I hear the word *gamification*, my blood starts to boil.

It's easy to sympathize with the impulse for gamification. Just look at that kid absorbed in a video game! What if we harnessed that power of engagement for different purposes? Usually what results, unfortunately, are things like badges to earn, or goals to achieve, or some other gamelike structured experience. Gamification promises magic behavior modification through reward and punishment, a silver bullet to get people to do what you want.

Here's the rub. In strip mining the superficial aspects of games—points, levels, and rewards—gamification leaves the soul of play behind. All of the most valuable experiences of games—the transgressive creativity of play, the delicate dance of desire and meaning, the critical leverage of thinking in systems—evaporates when games become instrumentalized as vehicles for memorizing or weaponized as frequent-flyer reward programs. Any approach to design implies an intrinsic model of what it means to be human. The model for gamification? It's a rat in a cage. A Skinnerian behaviorist fantasy.

Field-defining scholars who study games and learning, like James Gee, Constance Steinkhuler, and Kurt Squire, view any well-designed game as intrinsically valuable. Games can engender communities of learning, they can help us think rigorously, they provide contexts where we can learn how to learn. Yet the gamification of education too often treats games like injectors of curricular information: games exist to deliver data more efficiently. This approach replicates today's unfortunate trend of test-driven factual knowledge—the absolutely lowest form of learning—and has nothing to do with how education can address the complex challenges facing the world today.

It's like reducing cuisine to nutrition. Try and convince a passionate chef that everything about food—the aesthetics, the history, the culture, the conversation around a meal—should all be boiled off to focus on how food can be a vehicle for vitamins and minerals. Certainly, nutrition is a part of cuisine, but I would not want to live in a world where the experience of food was flattened into a functional regime of "nutrification."

In saying games can be justified only if they do good or fix the world, we turn a blind eye to the beauty, the power, the mystery of games as they already are. We can learn from the field of art education about how to connect learning to aesthetic works of culture. As I have come to understand from my art educator parents Gilbert Clark and Enid Zimmerman, art teachers don't try and measure the information gleaned from exposure to a painting. They see art as a part of critical contexts for the exchange of ideas. Looking at, talking about, and making art are all part of being human.

Scrambling after the seductive promises of gamification is part of a larger cultural trend. The economist's version of reality—humans as rational actors and inexorable growth as the measure of success—has become the default way to explain the world. But it's not the only option. Anyone who studies decision-making (including game designers) knows that people are more complicated than instrumental rationality and behaviorist psychology might lead you to believe. Ask yourself: What is your design's intrinsic model for what it means to be human?

THE STRUCTURE OF PROBLEMS

In a zero-sum game, when I win, you lose. This traditional structure is just one way of engineering a game's system, and it has implications for the world outside of games.

One classical game structure is the model of a zero-sum game. The term *zero sum* refers to the fact that any gains at the end are equaled exactly by losses. The winner's victory is balanced by the loser's defeat. Most games are zero-sum: a Soccer match, an arcade fighting game, even an evening of Poker among friends, in which the sum of extra money that some players pocket equals the amount that others have lost.

It sounds brutal, but it's not a horrible model for a game. There is an elegance to the zero-sum structure, a mirrorlike transitiveness. It heightens the stakes for the contest. As you dance with your opponent, every step forward is someone else's step back.

But it's not the only tool in the toolbox. There are plenty of other models for structuring the contest of a game. In the cooperative board game Pandemic (2008), everyone wins or loses together against the game-controlled antagonist of a global disease. In tabletop role-playing games, there is typically no winning or losing—the goal is to keep the game going, to tell better stories, to explore strange new worlds. In games like *Minecraft* (2011), in which players devise levels for others to play, there might be more of a gift

economy, as everyone shares in the benefits of the creativity of the other players.

Moving beyond zero-sum thinking means recognizing the hidden parts of systems that end up contributing to zero-sum structures. Some are very explicit, like the rules of the game that define winning and losing. Others are embedded in our conceptions of what is fair and the cultural narratives that justify the systems we help perpetuate.

In *The Sum of Us* (2021), writer and activist Heather McGhee applies the concept of zero-sum thinking to politics and culture. She describes the ongoing zero-sum narrative in the United States—the idea that when some benefit, it always comes at a cost to others. Through this distorted lens, affirmative action or social welfare means that some lose when others gain. She ties this narrative to the history of racism in the United States. In one poignant example, McGhee traces the way public pools either closed or became privatized once they were mandated to admit everyone. A public good was shuttered because those in power felt it shouldn't be shared.

The result of zero-sum thinking is widespread systemic inequity. For example, redlining neighborhoods and preventing home ownership for Black Americans has had snowball effects in perpetuating cycles of poverty for generations. McGhee's point is that the racism of zero-sum thinking negatively affects our entire society. Despite the fact that the United States has the resources to eliminate domestic poverty, the narrative that helping some disadvantages others has led to policies that perpetuate inequality.

To paraphrase game designer Mitu Khandaker, systems thinking is necessary but not sufficient. The toolbox of systems literacy must be infused with deeply human values and a deeply critical perspective. Otherwise, even the best intentions might not escape the zero-sum narrative. There are other stories we can tell. Stories that might shift the culture and spin out new policies. Those policies need to be designed too—they are just going to rely on different kinds of systems to get to their results. How might we redesign— for example—the vast game of capitalism for the better? We need to leverage the benefits and insights of a systems-based approach to understanding the world, even as we recognize its limits and move beyond them.

EXERCISES
WHEN YOU HAVE A COUPLE OF HOURS TO TINKER WITH A SYSTEM

MODDING TIC-TAC-TOE

Take the classic game of Tic-Tac-Toe, change some rules, and see what happens. An introduction to modifying, designing, and communicating game systems.

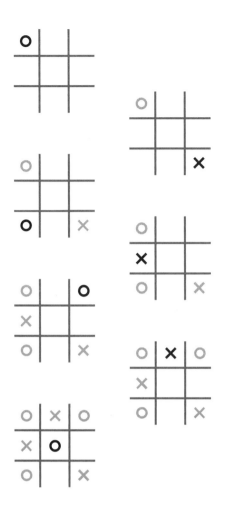

What You Need

- Any number of players, working in pairs, in person or remotely online
- 45–60 minutes
- Writing and drawing supplies
- Prototyping materials (optional)

What You Learn

- Understanding rules and modifying them to change the experience of play
- The iterative design process of experimentation and playtesting
- Communicating a design by writing out its rules

1. Establish the rules of the game

Start by drawing a game of Tic-Tac-Toe on a whiteboard. Then ask what the rules of Tic-Tac-Toe are. What do we need to know in order to play? Brainstorm the rules together by having people shout out suggestions. You will likely end up with something like this:

- Play takes place on a 3 × 3 grid
- 2 players play together
- Players alternate placing an X or an O on an empty square
- 3-in-a-row of the same symbol is a win for that player
- If neither player can make a move, the game ends in a draw

Note that rules of good strategic play (play in the center first or block if your opponent is about to win) are different from the actual game rules. You can play the game badly and ignore good strategy but still play correctly by the rules.

Discuss: How do logical rules become a system of play?

Think of rules as a kind of language. Every game of Tic-Tac-Toe that has ever been played—whether on a classroom whiteboard or by drawing lines with sticks on a beach—has followed these rules. The rules form the grammar for speaking the language of Tic-Tac-Toe. It's staggering to think about the billions of hours of behavior that the simple rules of Tic-Tac-Toe have generated.

Discuss: Is Tic-Tac-Toe fair?

Yes, it is fair in that the 2 players follow the same rules in the same way. At the same time, no, it's not really fair because whoever goes first has a strong advantage. Or, perhaps, if every game ends in a draw, it actually doesn't matter who goes first.

SYSTEM DYNAMICS

MODDING TIC-TAC-TOE

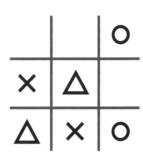

2. What can we change?

Have the group brainstorm a list of possible changes that could deepen, expand, or just mix up the game. That might include things like:

- size or shape of the grid
- winning conditions
- types of symbols you can draw
- where and how you can place a symbol
- permanence of symbols (maybe you can move them or erase them)
- number of players
- available time on your turn

Think about: Design intent

Beyond just changing the game for the sake of changing it, what is a larger goal that could help guide a redesign? For example, making Tic-Tac-Toe more exciting, or strategically deeper, or, conversely, more random and arbitrary. Perhaps it could be possible to make the game fairer by taking away first-mover advantage. Or the opposite: leaning into the game's asymmetrical inequality and intentionally make it less fair.

Think about: Changing the story

Beyond the structural aspects of the game—the abstract, formal elements—are there other things that could be modified? For example, what about the content or narrative of Tic-Tac-Toe? What happens if the classic "noughts and crosses" are replaced with cats and dogs? Or cops and protestors? Are the 2 players given identities or roles of some kind? One way to spin this entire exercise is to focus on how a mod of Tic-Tac-Toe might embody or depict unfairness, inequality, or oppression.

3. Mod the game

Have designers work in pairs (a group of 3 is OK—they can try out a mod for 3 players). Because the groups will be paired up later on, arrange things so that you will have an even number of groups.

They should try out their rule-change ideas by actually playing their own new versions of the game—as soon as possible. If you do have physical materials on hand—movable tokens, 6-sided dice. stackable blocks, sticky notes—encourage players to use them! Physical affordances will suggest new play mechanics.

Think about: How to shut up and play

This is key. Help the designers fight the tendency to discuss and debate ideas in the abstract instead of trying them out and seeing how they work in practice. Encourage them to stop talking and start playing. Each group should grab the first idea that comes up and just play it out. Then quickly discuss what happened, make adjustments, and play again. This cyclical process is the essence of iterative design.

Think about: Modifying only a rule or two at a time

As they settle into an iterative process, it's best to change something small and see what happens. If you change too much all at once, it's difficult to determine which changes are affecting the play in what ways.

4. Write out new rules

Once everyone has a somewhat playable new version, pause their design processes. Have each pair of designers write out the rules of their new version of the game on paper. Tell them to make a complete set of rules, written for a player who knows nothing about how to play the game.

Encourage them to be as explicit as possible, including diagrams and illustrations, if needed. This is a chance for them to practice the crucial design skill of communication.

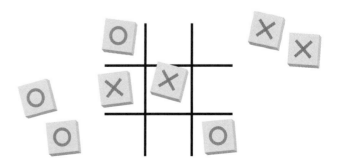

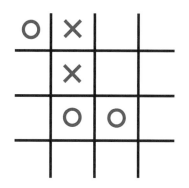

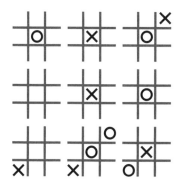

5. Painful playtesting

Pair up the groups, so that each team is assigned to another team. The 2 paired groups will play each other's games.

One of the groups in each pair watches silently while the other group tries to play the first group's game by only reading and following the written rules. The designers are absolutely forbidden from trying to verbally explain their games to each other. Be very strict about this! See if the rules alone can explain the games. If players are confused, don't help them—wait and see if they can muddle through, even if they get some details wrong. If players are completely stuck, designers can help explain, but the goal is to realize how difficult it is to communicate rules well.

When the playtest is done, it's the other group's turn. Now the former playtesters get to see their own game being played while they watch in painful silence. Everyone should have a chance to playtest someone else's game and a chance to see their own game being played.

Discuss: As a player, share something you experienced

Rather than have each group share what they *designed*, ask participants to talk about the game they *played*. What was unexpected or engaging about the mod they experienced? Having people talk about designs made by others, rather than going methodically around the room as each group makes a "design presentation," makes for a more spontaneous discussion.

Discuss: As a designer, whose game was understood perfectly?

Ask for a show of hands to see whose game was not played exactly according to the intended rules. Silently looking over someone's shoulder as your design is being misunderstood is very difficult! But it's absolutely essential practice in the meditation-under-the-waterfall discipline of nonintrusive playtesting.

Discuss: Were there any misunderstandings that led to new ideas?

Accidents and confusion can be creatively productive. It may be that some of the playtesters stumbled upon interesting new ways to play. Did this happen to anyone?

Context

Anyone can modify Tic-Tac-Toe and immediately experience how small changes in rules can produce unexpected results—there are so many ways to mod even this simple game. In a short amount of time, this exercise can encapsulate the entire design process: analyzing a system, prototyping and trying out changes, communicating to players, and even observational playtesting. For more Tic-Tac-Toe modding inspiration, see chapter 5 of *The Well-Played Game* (1978) by Bernie DeKoven, where he offers a glorious avalanche of ways to change the game. Long live Tic-Tac-Toe!

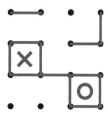

SYSTEM DYNAMICS

DIE VS. DIE

A simple game:
roll 2 dice and the
higher number wins.
What happens when
you design your
own custom dice?
An exercise in
competitive probability.

0. Gather materials

Die vs. Die needs a handful of materials:

- a regular 6-sided die for each participant

- a blank die for each participant

- whiteboard markers for writing on the blank dice

- small tokens in 2 colors (25–30 total for each participant)

You can find blank dice in game hobby stores or online. It's also possible to make blank dice by using masking tape or sticky labels to cover up the sides of regular dice.

The small tokens can be in more than 2 colors, as long as when the designers are paired up, each designer in a pair has about 25 or 30 tokens that are all the same color but a different color from their partner.

Each pair of participants will also need a copy of the board on the top half of the Die vs. Die game sheet on page 184. If you are running the optional bonus step of the exercise, each individual participant will need a deck of numbers 1–6. You can print and cut the cards from the bottom half of the game sheet, or you can make a deck by simply writing numbers on index cards. (Just be sure the numbers don't show through to the back!)

What You Need

- Any number of players, working in pairs, in person or remotely online

- 60–90 minutes

- 6-sided dice

- Blank dice (small cubes)

- Whiteboard markers for writing on the blank dice

- A large number of small tokens in 2 or more colors

- Game sheet, page 184

What You Learn

- Common misconceptions about how randomness works

- Techniques for visualizing probability

- How to meaningfully incorporate chance into design

SYSTEM DYNAMICS

DIE VS. DIE

1. Talk about luck

I like to start with this trick that I learned from game designer Richard Garfield. Draw or display 2 lines of 1s and 0s that look something like this:

1011111011111101111101000000111011111

0101010010101010101001011010101011011

Then ask: If the 1s and 0s represent coin flips (heads and tails), which row represents something closer to an actual series of coin flips?

Many people will pick the bottom row, with its fairly even distribution of heads and tails. The twist is that the top row, with long runs of the same number, is actually a much more typical kind of pattern.

Think about: Clumps of luck

When you are flipping a coin, there's always a 50 percent chance—a very big chance!—that the next flip will be the same as the last one. This means you are very likely to get long runs of the same symbol. It also means that in a small set of flips, you will almost never get half heads and half tails! Only with very large numbers of flips (hundreds, or thousands, or millions) will things even out to 50/50.

Think about: Story problems

If you have the time and inclination, talking through (and visualizing) tricky probability brainteasers can be a good warm-up for Die vs. Die. For example, the Two Daughters Problem or the Monte Hall Problem. *The Jungles of Randomness* (1997) by Ivars Peterson is a great source for more.

Never forget to comment on the cultural problematics of some of these math problems. For example, the Two Daughters Problem relies on a binary idea of gender. And in any case, why is it "two daughters" and not "two sons?"

2. Play the basic game and chart out the possibilities

Pair everyone up with a partner. To begin, make sure each designer has a regular 6-sided die. You and your partner each roll a die, and the higher roll wins. On a tie, nobody wins. (What a simple game!) A couple of practice duels will get the basic idea across.

To visualize the odds of this extremely straightforward game, the players will use the grid on the printout and the small tokens. One player will be using the white die numbers across the top, and the other will use the black die numbers along the side. Here's how it works:

- Both players roll their dice. For example, the player using white rolls a 1 and the player using black rolls a 4.

- Find the square on the chart that corresponds to the roll. A white 1 + a black 4 indicates the square on the left column (the 1 column) to the right of the 4. (It's a little like the game Battleship.)

- Put a marker there depending on who won—since the black number is higher, black won. So the black token is placed on the spot. If nobody wins, leave it blank.

Keep playing and a pattern will start emerging. After several rolls, you can tell everyone to stop rolling and just place their tokens to fill in the rest of the blanks. The resulting grid shows you which die wins in each possible combination of rolls—the universe of every possible match that might ever happen in this simple game. Because the 2 dice are the same, the number of wins for each color—the black and white tokens—appear an equal number of times.

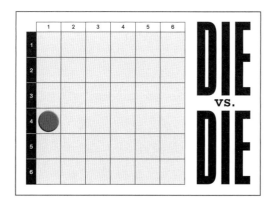

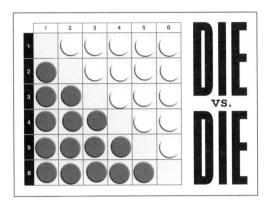

Think about: Tactile numbers

Yes, as probability statistics, this is very elementary stuff. The point of this exercise is not to dive into advanced mathematics. It is to use tactile and visual means to develop a gut sense for what probability *feels* like. This exercise uses different ways of looking at numbers (rolling dice, placing tokens, looking at rows of 1s and 0s). Hopefully, one approach will speak to an individual participant.

3. Design custom dice

Now the fun starts. The real game of Die vs. Die requires each player to design their own custom die. You'll be using the blank dice for this—each player will need their own individual blank die.

Each player designs their own custom die in secret and writes the numbers on the sides. Here are the rules to follow for creating the custom dice:

- the 6 faces must add to exactly 21, just like a regular die (1+2+3+4+5+6 = 21)

- each side must be a positive whole number (no fractions, decimals, negative numbers)

- it is OK to use 0 as a number on one or more sides

- the numbers can repeat (the number on a face does not need to be unique)

- some sample custom dice:

    0-2-3-4-5-7   0-0-0-7-7-7   1-1-2-2-3-12

4. Play with custom dice against your partner

Using their newly designed custom dice, the partners play against each other. The game is the same: roll both dice and the higher roll wins. Have them battle for 10 rolls, and keep track on a scratch piece of paper who won each roll (or if there was a tie).

Then ask the group if there is a way to see which die is actually better than the other one—at least in terms of which is more likely to win a random match. The answer is to use the chart, of course! The grid of odds that was used for the 2 standard dice can be used for the custom dice too.

They can cross out the 1, 2, 3, 4, 5, 6 along the top and side—and replace those numbers with the custom numbers of their 2 dice in ascending order. Then there's no need to roll; just use the tokens to mark which die would win each combination. Fill out the chart with tokens. It might look something like this:

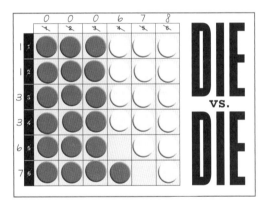

Which die beats which die? If each token represents a victory for that color, you can just count the tokens. In this case, black (with 19 tokens on the chart) beats white more often (with just 15).

Then, ask everyone to compare the record of their 10 random battles to the results in the chart. Likely, some pairs will have had results that mirrored the probabilities in their chart. Others almost certainly did not. What gives?

SYSTEM DYNAMICS

DIE VS. DIE

5. Expand the discussion

Likely there are 1 or 2 designers in the group who had a particularly strong die against their opponent. So they might think they have made the perfect Die vs. Die die. It's time to burst their bubbles!

Ask for 2 volunteers who think they have unbeatable dice and chart out their die numbers on a whiteboard or on one of the grids using tokens. It will reveal which die has a better shot at beating the other.

With the 2 dice charted out, what numbers can be tweaked to turn the tables so that the losing die wins? It's all about changing the numbers to use them *efficiently* against your opponent—there's no need to beat the other die's numbers by more than 1 point. In the example on the previous page, if the white die's 0s were turned into 1s or 2s, they would get the edge on the black die's lower numbers. As long as enough numbers stay above 3, the white die can eke out a win.

Discuss: Is there a single die that is better (on average) than any other?

Is there, in fact, one die to rule them all? There may be a die design that has better chances against a majority of other possible dice. But, in fact, the value of a die in Die vs. Die is not whether it mathematically averages out better than other dice given millions of theoretical matches. The value of a die is how it does at this particular moment, against the opponent right in front of you.

Discuss: What other systems feature this kind of constantly evolving "metagame?"

The process of adjusting your die to get an edge over different opponents is a simple analog for the many kinds of customizable systems we see today, from deck-building card games and character-drafting eSports to the strategic jockeying of the stock-market or social media stats. Complex systems support this kind of evolution in which a part of the game involves tweaking and modifying your capabilities over time.

Discuss: Why didn't everyone's wins and losses mirror the probabilities on the chart?

The reason why many of the groups did not get wins and losses that correspond to the odds on the chart is because of the small sample size. Like the coin flips, with only 10 battles, you are not going to have nearly enough outcomes to start matching the overall odds reflected on the grid. The challenge of designing games with this in mind is that your players will very likely not be playing your game thousands or millions of times. The 10 real battles are all they might ever experience.

Discuss: Does randomness make a game better or worse?

What does luck feel like? It depends. Chance is a paradox. It can add excitement and uncertainty to a game, giving players who are behind a sense of agency and an opportunity to catch up. It can also do just the opposite: it can rob players of agency by placing their entire destiny in the hands of fate. On the other hand, once you come to understand how randomness works in a particular game, it can become just another system to tinker with. Greg Costikyan's *Uncertainty in Games* (2013) dives deep into these paradoxes.

6. Optional: a deck of numbers

To explore the permutations of chance from a slightly different angle, feel free to add this additional step to the exercise. Print onto card stock and cut out the deck of cards numbered 1–6 that are on the Die vs. Die game sheet (or make your own with index cards). Each participant needs their own deck.

Have them pair up with their original partner again and play the basic Die vs. Die game, but this time, instead of rolling a regular die, they will draw cards from their decks. Once you draw and play a card, leave it out on the table. You'll play 6 rounds. By the very last round, you'll know exactly the cards that you and your opponent are going to draw.

Then play one last variation of the game. Use the cards 1–6, but instead of shuffling them into a deck, turn them into a hand of cards. So rather than a random draw, each player can *choose* which card to play from their hand of 6. Play through 6 rounds of this version, leaving cards played out on the table, until both players' hands are empty.

Discuss: How are dice different than cards?

There is a fundamental difference between rolling a die and drawing a random card. When you roll a die, the next roll still preserves the complete set of possible outcomes. Cards are different. When you draw a card, that card is taken out of the possible outcomes for the next turn (unless you shuffle it in again). It's a bit like the difference between a renewable resource, like solar energy, and a nonrenewable resource, like fossil fuels, that is gradually used up. Each has different implications for the kinds of randomness they can imbue in a system. There are other differences too. For example, on a tactile level of experiential ritual, the feeling of a bouncing random die is very different than revealing the next hidden card from the deck.

Discuss: How was a random card different than choosing a card?

How did the 2 card-based versions of the game feel, compared to each other? Perhaps the choice-based version was more strategic and psychological. Maybe the random draw was a bit more exciting and unexpected. Both of them had the feature of the final turn being a foregone conclusion—did that final inevitability feel satisfying and dramatic or arbitrary and anticlimactic? There are complex aesthetic and emotional implications to what seem like fairly dry decisions about how to embody a random algorithm.

Discuss: How does randomness in Tetris work?

Randomness in games is not random—it is designed. In a game like Tetris, you will see thousands of pieces over many plays. Remembering the coin-flip patterns, you want to control randomness so that you don't get long strings of the same piece. The most common approach is to put the 5 kinds of Tetris pieces into a virtual bag, with 2 copies of each piece. That limits the same piece being drawn in a row to 4 (2 long Tetris pieces at the very end of a bag and 2 long Tetris pieces at the very beginning of the next bag). Why would you want 2 of each piece in the bag, and not 1 or 10?

Context

Die vs. Die brings together a host of issues surrounding randomness and makes them tactile and intuitive. And fun! This exercise is a version of Dice Wars by Stone Librande, a game designer who has created many brilliant and elegant activities for teaching design. Stone's approach—using games to teach design—has been tremendously influential on my thinking and in the game industry and in academia as well. Download Stone's talks and exercises at Stonetronix.com.

GET OUT!

How can our heroine Ute escape?
Design spatial logic challenges
of increasing complexity to unlock
the poetics of puzzles.

0. Preparation

To get things ready, you'll need to print the game sheet pages as listed below. Participants will be working in groups of 2.

Puzzle Grid (page 185)
3 per group

Design Worksheets (186)
3-5 per group

Game Elements (187)
1 per group

Game Pieces (188)
2 or more copies on card stock

Sample Puzzle (189)
1 copy only (for you to use as a demo)

For the game pieces, 2 copies is good for about 3-4 pairs of designers; 4 copies will give you supplies for about a dozen participants (working in 6 pairs). You'll need to cut out each of the little square game pieces, which can be a little fussy—sorry about that! (A paper cutter comes in very handy.) I recommend putting each type of piece into a different small envelope to keep them organized for the next time you run the exercise.

One final tip: the two rows of Ute pieces—the pairs of smiling faces—should not be cut apart; instead fold them to make a piece that will stand up on the table. They'll be much easier to move around that way.

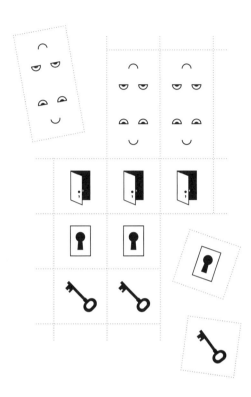

What You Need

- Any number of players, working in pairs
- 90–120 minutes
- Game sheets, pages 185–189

What You Learn

- Fundamentals of puzzle and level design
- Designing efficiently and expressively with modular elements
- How to teach players new concepts and gradually ramp up challenge

SYSTEM DYNAMICS

GET OUT!

1. Explain the core game

Gather everyone around a central table and explain how the basic interaction works. In Get Out! our somewhat single-minded heroine Ute is trapped. All she wants is to reach the exit.

Lay the sample level page on the table and put an Ute piece (the smiling face) on the starting X. Ute always begins on an X and wins when she reaches an exit square with a door. Here's the hitch. Ute is very determined. She can move only in a straight line, and she keeps going in that direction until she hits a wall. So she can't stop and turn in place—she can only choose where to go after she hits a wall and stops moving. For example, here's one way Ute can get to the exit in the sample puzzle:

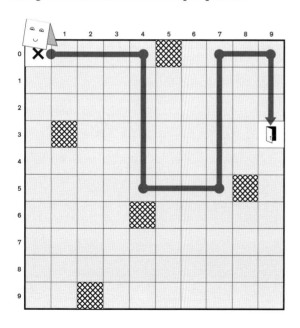

There's actually another way for Ute to get out that uses only 5 moves instead of 6. Can anyone find it?

2. Design basic puzzles

Now it's time for each pair of designers to put together a puzzle or two. Each group gets:

- a large blank puzzle grid
- an Ute piece
- an X starting piece
- an Exit door piece
- several solid Walls that act to block Ute (no special pieces yet!)

Give the designers about 10 or 12 minutes to design, using only these basic components to try and create an interesting experience for a player. If it helps, the design worksheets (with 4 grids on a page) can be used to sketch out ideas. The challenge is to create something genuinely unexpected. If a group finishes early, they can design a second puzzle level.

Think about: Authoring solutions

A traditional puzzle has a "correct answer" that the player is trying to figure out. (Think about how a crossword puzzle or a brainteaser riddle works.) When you are designing a puzzle, you are in a sense designing—and then hiding—the answer that the player will try to sleuth out.

Think about: The aha! moment

The pleasure of solving puzzles often comes during a moment of insight when you are able to look at the parts of the system in a new way and shift your thinking to arrive at a creative solution. The challenge in this stage of the exercise—and to be honest it's really difficult!—is to create an aha moment using just the limited set of basic elements (Start, Exit, Wall). Can it be done?

3. Play and discuss basic puzzles

Once each group has a puzzle or two completed, designers walk around the room and play each other's puzzles. Depending on the overall size of the group, it's OK if everyone doesn't have a chance to play every single puzzle—the main point is to get a good sampling of what the others have done.

Then it's time to discuss. Rather than talk about their own designs, have them comment on puzzles by other designers that they just played.

Discuss: Did anyone's puzzle use spatial logic in an interesting way?

One of the tricky wrinkles of the Get Out! puzzle mechanic is that Ute can be physically near the exit but very far away from it in terms of number of required moves. (Or vice versa—located very far from the exit but only a move or two away.) Did any of the designs tease the player with these aspects of the space design, perhaps by starting Ute very close to the exit?

Discuss: Were there any puzzles that played with the "canvas" of the grid?

Even elements that might not be directly part of the core puzzle logic become important for the player experience. What's the difference in *feeling* between symmetrical, logical layouts and random, chaotic puzzle spaces? What about spaces that are mostly empty air versus spaces that are all filled in with walls?

Discuss: What makes these puzzles meaningful? Were there any aha moments?

The Get Out! puzzles are like structural poems that use a very limited vocabulary to shape their meaning. Each puzzle rearranges the linguistic elements of Start, Exit, Walls—and blank squares, of course!—in different ways. What rhythms and sensibilities emerge? By seeing many puzzles together side by side, it's possible to start appreciating the subtle differences of expression in each one.

Think about: Overcoming functional fixedness

The rule-breaking mindset needed to figure out the answer to a puzzle is similar to overcoming what psychologists call *functional fixedness*, which is thinking about using things only in a conventional way. The following is a classic functional fixedness puzzle: Can you mount a candle on a wall, using only a box of matches and some tacks? The candle can't be stuck to the wall with the tacks or melted onto the wall. But you can tack the matchbox to the wall and use it as a little sconce for the candle. It's a nice puzzle design that requires you to think about using objects in unexpected ways, as the matchbox *container* is transformed into a *shelf*.

Think about: Adding expert goals

One approach to generating different layers of challenge is to embed extra, more advanced goals into a single puzzle. For example, the Get Out! sample puzzle has a solution that can be completed in 6 moves and a less obvious 5-move solution. Designers are free to include an expert goal in the Get Out! puzzles they make, in the form of a target number of moves. The basic goal is just getting out; the expert goal is doing so within the move limit. If they add an expert goal, they should write the target number of moves in the Notes section at the bottom of the puzzle page.

SYSTEM DYNAMICS

GET OUT!

— GAME ELEMENTS —

 Ute

She moves in a straight line and stops when she hits something

 Exit

Move Ute to this square to GET OUT and beat the level

 Locked Door

Door that requires a key; acts like a wall when locked

 Key

Ute needs to touch this to unlock a door; she stops when she hits it

 Wall

This stops Ute from moving

 Breakable Wall

Ute stops like it's a normal wall, but then the breakable wall disappears

4. Brainstorm new elements

Now it's time to give the designers a little more to work with. The Game Elements sheet lists all of the various pieces that designers might put into a level. Lead everyone through a brainstorm session about what some of these elements might do. Restrict the brainstorm to simple, static elements that are placed on the grid. Some Get Out! elements I have seen in the past include:

- sticky spots that stop Ute's movement and let her move in any direction

- conveyor belts that move Ute automatically in a particular direction

- pairs of teleporters that instantly teleport Ute between them

- coins or points that can be optionally collected as part of an expert goal

- keys that need to be picked up in order to unlock doors

- breakable walls that are removed when Ute runs into them

- hazards that eliminate Ute if she collides with them

- shields that protect Ute from the next hazard she encounters

As they brainstorm these elements, write down what they do on a central Game Elements page or on a whiteboard. You definitely don't need to fill up the entire sheet. Defining 5 or 6 elements is plenty.

Think about: Getting specific

Be sure to describe each new element in enough detail for everyone to understand how it works in exactly the same way. For example, if Ute has to move over a key to pick it up and unlock a door, does she stop when she encounters a key? Or does she pass over a key and scoop it up? Or perhaps the player chooses whether or not to stop and pick up the key. Record these details on the Elements sheet or on a whiteboard.

Think about: Keeping it simple

Designers love to overdesign. Don't let the group go overboard with complicated elements, like hazards with autonomous movement or monsters with intricate combat rules. Keep things as simple as possible! The challenge of this phase of the exercise is to see how even very simple elements can be combined in modular ways to produce complexity. (There will be a chance for more complex elements later on.)

5. Design advanced puzzles

Now let them start designing. Each group selects 1 or 2 special elements only—and no more! They will be designing with the basic elements (Start, Exit, Walls) plus their selected 1 or 2 elements. Each group designs:

- 1 *tutorial level* that introduces a player to how the elements work

- 1 or 2 *complex levels* that leverage the elements for additional challenge.

A few important design tips:

- *Number each puzzle.* Use the # sign in the corner of the puzzle-grid page to number each level so that it is clear in what order they should be played.

- *Mark starting positions.* If there are dynamic elements, like a key that can get picked up, mark the starting location so that the puzzle can be easily reset.

- *Expert goals are OK.* If they want to add expert goals in any of the levels, mark them in the Notes section at the bottom of the page.

SYSTEM DYNAMICS

GET OUT!

6. Play and discuss advanced puzzles

They should be able to put their puzzles together in 10 or 15 minutes. Then it's time to share. As before, designers move through the room and play each other's designs. Remember to have players reset any puzzles back to the starting state after they play (if there are any dynamic elements that can change).

When the designers have gotten a sampling of each other's levels, bring everyone together for a group discussion. As before, have them focus on their experience of others' puzzles rather than explaining their own designs.

Discuss: Which sets of puzzle tutorials taught particularly well (or poorly)?

The idea of teaching the player—creating a tutorial level to teach something new—is an incredibly central design concept. Every design is a kind of language, and every designer is an educator who has to teach this language to their audience. How did the Get Out! tutorial designs approach the challenge of teaching players something new?

Discuss: Which puzzles seemed to have a balanced difficulty?

Difficulty often comes up as a topic when puzzles get complex. Why does one puzzle feel crushingly hard while another feels seductively challenging? What is the ineffable tipping point when rote tasks become intriguing enigmas? Don't assume that harder is better! If you do want to make crushingly challenging puzzles, one design approach is to use short-term goals to lead players through to the end. Providing some early wins (picking up a key, finishing even if it's not within the export goal limit) can help maintain player interest through harder challenges.

Discuss: Which puzzles captured your interest and attention and why?

Puzzles are wonderful case studies in shaping player pleasure through challenge, frustration, and reward. This dance of desire emerges as puzzles tease the player with the promise of an answer that remains hidden—until it isn't. Have the designers reflect on how and why certain Get Out! levels tickled their fancy and others did not. Becoming attuned to one's own sense of pleasure is an important part of being a designer.

Discuss: Which puzzles transcended the page?

When you use any kind of level design editor or technical tool, the hope is to rise above the typical and expected. Like a poet using language to express things beyond words, the key is using modular elements in careful and surprising ways. Did any of the puzzles offer a mind-expanding moment when playing it somehow transcended the puzzle itself?

Discuss: Do we have to agree on which puzzles worked better than others?

No! There may well be serious disagreement among the group about which puzzles were more enjoyable. That's OK. Pleasure is subjective, and we shouldn't expect everyone to have the same taste. Should designers target narrow kinds of players or aim for broader audiences?

Context

The secret of Get Out! is the enforced simplicity of the puzzles. It's always delightful to see how expressive and wide-ranging the designs can be, even with a radically limited vocabulary of parts. Get Out! is inspired directly by classic puzzle games like *Sokoban* (1981) and *Pengo* (1982), and it offers a kind of literacy by exposing designers to species of systems they might not normally encounter. It may be that some are turned on to go deeper into structural puzzle design, while others realize how much they really don't like sliding-block puzzles. Both are equally valid and equally useful reactions to Get Out!

7. Optional: go deeper

Two rounds of design (first basic and then advanced puzzles) are plenty! If you have additional time, however, the exercise can be extended to let the designers explore the design possibility space even farther. For this optional third round, each group of designers gets to choose one of the following:

- *Go deep.* Stick with their existing elements and design more puzzle levels.

- *Add an element.* Mix in one more game element, and make more levels.

- *Change a basic rule.* For example, the walls wrap around, *Asteroids*-style.

- *Add a dynamic procedure.* For example, an enemy that responds to Ute's movement or elements that are placed randomly each time you play.

This final optional stage opens the barn doors and lets the designers run a bit wild. However, remind them to keep things simple. The rule of thumb is that if any new element cannot be explained with a few written notes on the puzzle sheet, it is too complicated to include.

Also, don't forget to have them teach through design. Gently introduce any new elements through tutorial puzzles. It's OK to have several levels that link together in sequence. Be thoughtful about which concepts come first and remember to number them sequentially.

After another 10 or 15 minutes (or much longer, if you have the time), let everyone play each other's puzzles. The postgame discussion can be structured in a similar way as before.

SYSTEM DYNAMICS

UTOPIA 2099

A 2-player dice game about rebuilding society after a global catastrophe. Balancing the rules of this very simple system is surprisingly hard.

What You Need

- Any number of players, working in pairs, in person or remotely online

- 60–90 minutes

- Game sheet, page 190 (1 copy per pair of designers)

- Writing utensils

- Two 6-sided dice per designer

- Optional: small tokens (10 per designer)

What You Learn

- Balancing a game system through iteration and experimentation

- How a system with very strong randomness can still be meaningful

- Rules and procedures as a means of depicting narrative characters

1. Play the basic game

Divide into pairs and give each pair a printout of the top half of the Utopia 2099 game sheet. Each designer also needs a pair of 6-sided dice and a writing utensil.

Utopia 2099 takes place after a global climate catastrophe; each player is trying to find happiness for their tiny community among the dangers of civilization's collapse. The player who achieves enough happiness first wins. To keep track of their accumulated happiness, players can use small tokens (like chips or cubes) or keep track on pencil and paper.

To play, each player rolls their pair of dice simultaneously. Then consult the game sheet to see what happens. The dice are resolved in order from the lowest to the highest numbers. So, for example, any 1s are resolved before any 2s. Each die makes 1 action happen, depending on the numbers rolled.

An example: I rolled a 2 and a 4, and my opponent rolled a 5 and a 5. The 2 is an Artifact, which gives me 2 happiness points, and the 4 is a Wall, so I can defend against 1 Raid for this turn. My opponent's two 5s are then resolved—they are both Raids. I defend against 1 of their Raids with my Wall, but the other Raid is undefended, so I lose 1 happiness point.

You need 10 or more happiness points to win. The game ends if, after resolving all of the dice on a turn, one player has 10 or more happiness. Then the player with the most happiness wins. If both players have 10 or more happiness and they tie, then play another turn.

Talk everyone through a turn or two together to show them how the game works. A few helpful reminders for when you are teaching the game:

- Resolve actions in order from low to high numbers. So Thieves always act last.

- A Raid reduces a player's happiness total.

- The Thief actually steals happiness from one player and gives it to the other. (If your opponent doesn't have 3 happiness, you can only steal what they have.)

- If both players roll a Thief, they cancel each other out.

UTOPIA 2099

2. Discuss what happened

It should take only a few minutes to play through a full game. Once everyone has finished and you have resolved any questions about how the game works, it's time to talk about it.

Discuss: What aspects of the game are working and not working?

Walls are boring! Sure, but why? Because they happen so often relative to Armies, Walls don't feel valuable. They certainly feel less exciting than when the other actions come up.

Discuss: Anything else?

Thieves are overpowered! Yes, sneakily so! The Thief doesn't just give you a boost of 3—because one player's happiness goes down while the other's goes up, Thieves can create a difference of up to 6 happiness between the 2 players. This makes their influence far outweigh anything else in the game.

Discuss: What determines the pace of the game?

Some actions bring you closer to a conclusion, and some delay conclusion. How long is too long for the game to feel right? A simple game like Utopia 2099 should probably not drag out too many turns. At the same time, if you make it too short, you may rob the experience of dramatic excitement.

Discuss: Why isn't there any choice?

Someone may point out that the game actually has zero player decision-making. That's very true! What's interesting is how the game can still feel compelling to play, even if it is totally random. How is this possible? As Pachinko and Roulette demonstrate, sometimes the drama or intricacy of a system can sustain player interest, even without a decision-making structure.

Discuss: How strong is the role of randomness in the experience?

The roll of the dice is all that happens in Utopia 2099. Is it possible to tell which parts of the player experience are based on the designed structure and which parts emerge from the element of chance? Is the experience just a random jumble? Or can things be designed into a better shape?

3. Adjust the system

Armed with an analysis of the system, each pair of designers can start making changes in order to improve the game. They will be using the right side of the page (the section with dice followed by blank spaces) to write in their own look-up table for the dice rolling.

Here are the things they can change in order to adjust the system:

- Adjust any circled numbers for each action
- Change which numbers do what (make 1, 2, and 3 all Farms)
- Remove actions from the chart entirely (get rid of Walls)
- They cannot make up new actions or change the basic game logic
- The Thief must appear only one time and in slot 6
- Winning conditions (10 happiness) must remain the same

Let them start designing! Remember, both players in a pair will be sharing and using the same chart. You may have designers who are chomping at the bit to change the basic game rules, modify the winning conditions, or add choice in some way. Don't let them! Balancing within tight constraints is what this phase of the exercise is all about.

Think about: Designing through play

As always, don't let them talk and theorize too much before they start actually testing their ideas through play. The most important thing is to quickly implement a couple of changes and then playtest to see how it affects the overall balance.

Think about: Why they are making changes

Their goal for rebalancing the game is to change the experience for the better—whatever that means to them. Remind them of the problems that the group just brought up (boring Walls, overpowered Thieves, etc.), if they need some initial directions.

To Play

Each player rolls 2 dice.

Resolve lower numbers first, according to the dice chart.

Winning: at the end of a turn, if a player has 10+ happiness, the player with the most happiness wins the game (if it's a tie, play another turn).

■ **FARM**   +① happiness
■ **ARTIFACT** +② happiness
■ **WALL**   Defend ① Raid for this turn
■ **WALL**   Defend ① Raid for this turn
■ **RAID**   Opponent without wall loses ① happiness
■ **THIEF**   Steal ③ happiness from opponent

To Balance

Change any circled number.

Change which die numbers do which actions.

You can eliminate actions (i.e., no FARMS) but THIEF must stay only at 6.

No changes to core logic or rules for winning.

Utopia 2099

■ *FARM: +3 happiness*

■ *FARM: +3 happiness*

■ *WALL: defend 2*

■ *RAID: opponent loses 1*

■ *RAID: opponent loses 1*

■ **THIEF**   Steal ② happiness from opponent

4. Discuss the rebalanced system

Give them 10 or 12 minutes to playtest and finalize their changes and then pause the frantic dice rolling. Have everyone bring their redesigned rule sheets to a central table where they can all be seen side by side.

Discuss: What were the most common approaches? The most uncommon?

There were probably some approaches that many of the designs took: nerf the power of the Thief or remove one of the Walls. Identify these commonsense fixes. Did anyone try anything stranger? I've seen groups boost happiness numbers so that a game only lasts for 2 or 3 rounds or give the Farms negative numbers so that there's more potential drama with each roll.

Discuss: How do changes result in a particular experience?

Be sure that everyone can appreciate the range of different approaches to finding proper system balance. There's definitely no right or wrong way to approach this design problem! It's very much a subjective aesthetic question: What is the experience you are trying to create with your system redesign? What changes to the system will result in that experience?

Discuss: Why can't they make more fundamental changes?

In a real game production process, it is always easier to tweak existing stats rather than invent new features and change basic rules. If you can fix a design problem by altering numbers in a spreadsheet array, it's going to be much easier than a solution that requires completely new code and interface design. By restricting very narrowly what they can do, the exercise simulates this kind of designing within tight constraints.

BALANCING SYSTEMS

It's OK if the Expert's powers are more powerful or consequential than the other "basic" actions on the chart, as long as they are all balanced with the other Experts. You can also let the groups completely redesign one of the Expert powers, as long as it meets the criteria above: balanced, enjoyable, and feels thematically right. Each pair will be doing their own separate balancing of the Experts.

5. Introduce experts

The final stage of this exercise opens up the game to Experts: new characters, each with a unique special power. Pass out a copy of the bottom half of the game sheet to each group.

Here's how the Experts work: before each game, each player picks a different Expert. The Expert is always in slot 6, and their power happens whenever a 6 is rolled. (The rest of the die numbers 1–5 make use of the newly balanced version that they just designed.)

Then let them start playtesting and balancing the set of Experts. Their goal is to:

- balance each Expert so that each has a similar chance of winning

- ensure that the Experts are enjoyable and exciting to play

- make sure they *feel* right—that the power matches the Expert's identity

Think about: Establishing a "pivot point"

It's difficult to keep the Experts balanced with each other if all of them keep on changing—each tweak has to be checked and rechecked against all of the others. A good technique is to hold one of the Experts as a fixed pivot point and balance all of the other Experts against it. The Thief is a good candidate for a pivot point—it has already been balanced to fit in with the set of basic actions and can serve as the standard by which the power level of the others is measured.

Think about: Procedural representation

In its modest way, Utopia 2099 Expert design touches on how the form and content of a game can intersect. Does the Spy's power feel like sneaky, clandestine subterfuge? Trying to make each Expert's power expressive of their narrative identity (that is, signification through a rule-defined dynamic process) is one of the ways that games can uniquely portray content.

Utopia 2099
Experts

To Play

Each player picks a different expert.

For numbers 1–5, use your balanced version.

A 6 means your expert power happens (two 6s means it happens twice).

To Balance

The power of the THIEF remains the same.

Modify any of the expert powers.

You can completely redesign one expert (except for the THIEF).

Criteria

Power balance (equal chances of winning).

Each one is enjoyable and exciting to play.

The ability feels right for the narrative identity.

THIEF	Steal ② happiness from opponent
HISTORIAN	Reroll both dice and take both actions
ENGINEER	~~Raid with a strength of 2 (opponent loses 2 happiness)~~ *next turn after rolling change 1 die to any number*
SPY	~~Next turn, opponent does not roll at all~~ *next turn, opponent rolls 1 die*

For a remote video situation

Utopia 2099 works well as an online exercise. If participants don't have dice at home, there are many online dice sites (try typing "roll a die" into a browser search). Rather than writing on paper sheets, designers (still working in pairs) can use a shared online document. Paste the following text into the document for them to use. Pairs of designers can modify their own version of the look-up table to balance the system.

For Phase 1:

1. FARM: +[1] happiness
2. ARTIFACT: +[2] happiness
3. WALL: defend [1] Raid for the turn
4. WALL: defend [1] Raid for the turn
5. RAID: an undefended opponent loses [1] happiness
6. THIEF: steal [3] happiness from opponent

For Phase 2:

HISTORIAN: reroll both of your dice and take both actions

ENGINEER: Raid with a strength of 2 (opponent loses 2 happiness)

SPY: next turn, opponent does not roll at all

For discussions, everyone can paste their rebalanced table into the central shared document so that they are easy for everyone to view and compare.

Context

Utopia 2099 emerged during the global pandemic out of need for a quick systems-balancing exercise for online classes. The exercise works just as well in person—all you really need are a couple pairs of dice. The core game is extremely easy and fast to play, in part because players never make any decisions. But that's also what makes it possible to rapidly iterate and immediately see the results of design changes. It's a wonderfully flexible exercise. For example, to take it one step deeper, ask every group to design a completely new set of Experts.

6. Wrap-up discussion

Give them another 10 or 12 minutes to design and then have everyone bring both of their sheets to a central table for a comparative talk. What are different approaches that groups took to balancing the Experts? Were any powers completely redesigned? Perhaps some of the new powers even added some kind of choice to the system.

Discuss: How does balancing this game apply to other kinds of systems?

A game like Utopia 2099 has a *heterogeneous structure*, in which diverse and unique special powers need to be balanced against each other. This is a common design problem in contemporary tabletop games and video games, from collectible card games to digital eSports. Balancing a heterogeneous structure has bigger implications too: in some ways, it is similar to balancing the roles and activities of a diverse social community or organization.

Discuss: What was unexpected about the design process?

The final results of each group's balancing are less important than the process that got them there. What did each group learn about the cyclical methodologies of analyzing, modifying, and playtesting? When you are tackling a challenging design problem, the main thing to focus on is not the final answer but the process that will move you forward.

BALANCING SYSTEMS

TROUBLE IN DODGE CITY

Outlaws, Sheriffs, Saloons, oh my! The real trouble in Dodge City is that this card game just isn't fun. Fix it with feedback loops, meaningful choice, and design iteration.

0. Setup

Trouble in Dodge City is a game for 3–5 players. Aim for groups of 4 players, but it's OK if some groups are slightly bigger or smaller. Each group will need:

- a copy of the rules (page 192)
- a deck of game cards (page 193)
- 10 tokens per player in the group

To make the deck of cards, print out the card page onto card stock and cut along the dotted lines. One page of cards provides enough cards for a group of 3–5. Shuffle each deck.

Each group will need a big pile of tokens—10 tokens per player in the group. The tokens can be any small object (Poker chips, small cubes, glass beads). Players do not need tokens of their own specific color—the tokens are just used to keep score, so it's OK if the tokens are different colors or shapes. You will want some extra tokens on hand, in case a group adds more tokens to the game later on as part of their redesign.

What You Need

- Any number of players, working in groups of 3–5
- 60–90 minutes
- 10 or more small tokens per individual participant
- Game sheets, pages 191–192

What You Learn

- Identifying and modifying dynamic system mechanics
- Balancing a game design to provide for meaningful player choice
- The iterative playtesting process

BALANCING SYSTEMS

TROUBLE IN DODGE CITY

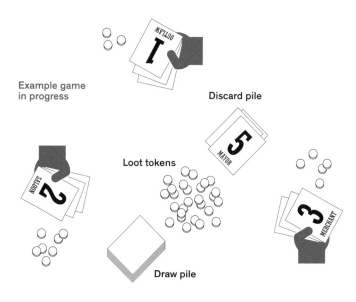

Example game in progress

Discard pile

Loot tokens

Draw pile

1. Demonstrate and play a game

Everyone gathers around a table to watch a group play a demonstration turn or two. Shuffle the cards and deal a hand of 3 cards to each player. (You can look at your hand but keep them hidden from other players.) The pile of tokens in the middle of the table represents all of the loot in Dodge City. The goal of the game is to end up with the most loot by the time the pile runs out.

Follow the rules on the game sheet. Going around the table in turns, each player will draw a card and then play a card from their hand. (Played cards are placed on a discard pile, which can be reshuffled if the deck runs out.) The 3, 4, and 5 cards (Merchant, Sheriff, and Mayor) are very straightforward—they give you that many tokens. The 1 card (Outlaw) lets you take 1 token from any other player you choose.

The 2 card (Saloon) is a little trickier. When you play a Saloon, you put it out in front of you and leave it there instead of discarding it. The next time your turn comes around, the Saloon will let you draw an extra card and play an extra card. Two Saloons out in front of you will let you draw 2 extra cards and play 2 extra cards.

The game is over as soon as the pile of tokens runs out—at that point count your tokens, and the player with the most tokens wins.

The demonstration group doesn't have to play a full game—a turn or two should be plenty to explain the basics. Get everyone back to their tables and have each group play through a full game.

2. Discuss the game

Trouble in Dodge City is not such a great game. Why? Start a discussion and try to figure it out.

Discuss: Does the game provide meaningful choices to players?

Not really. A core problem with the design is that it's pretty obvious what to do each turn. A 5 is always better than a 4, which is always better than a 3. An obvious choice is not an interesting or meaningful choice.

Discuss: Are there any snowball feedback loops in the game?

The Saloon card creates a positive or reinforcing feedback loop, also known as a snowball. The more Saloons you play, the more cards (including more Saloons) you get to play, which becomes a vicious cycle that can quickly run away with itself. It's very enjoyable to play Saloons, but it's just a matter of chance whether you draw them in the early game. Winning by that kind of pure luck is not particularly satisfying.

Discuss: What about any catch-up feedback loops?

The Outlaw card offers a negative or balancing feedback loop, also known as a catch-up mechanic. Because you presumably will take a token from the player with the most tokens (the person who is currently closest to winning), the action serves to level the playing field and helps players who are behind catch up. Yet it only shifts a total of 1 token, so it's really too weak to be very effective.

Discuss: What styles of play does the game encourage?

In tabletop strategy games, what are called "Euro-style" games de-emphasize direct interaction between players and instead are about being more efficient in how you use your resources. In contrast, so-called "Ameritrash-style" games let players directly interfere with each other, perhaps attacking or stealing resources. The Saloon (level yourself up in isolation, Euro-style) and the Outlaw (directly steal from another player, Ameritrash-style) each suggest different directions for the gameplay style. Yet because the overall design of Trouble in Dodge City is not working very well, the game isn't supporting either of these play styles very robustly.

Discuss: What determines the pace and length of the game?

Trouble in Dodge City has a steady ticking clock that ends the game—the diminishing central pile of loot tokens. Changing the size of this resource and how quickly it shrinks (or grows?) determines the length of the game. What does everyone think about the current length of the game? What would be better— a longer, slower strategic pace or a much faster lightning shoot-out?

3. Make some changes and playtest

Now that everyone has a sense of the design's current problems, it's time to try and fix them. Each group makes some changes to the game rules, by crossing off text on the rules sheet and writing in changes and additions.

What motivates their redesign? Modify something to make the game better. Remind them of the problems that you all just discussed. For example, when a player looks at their hand of cards and considers which card to play, it should feel like an *interesting choice*, and not like an obvious rote decision.

What aspects of the game might they change? It's up to them, but they might start with:

- Card actions—tweaking existing card powers or completely redesigning them

- Starting setup—the number of tokens in the game, the number of cards in your hand

- What happens on a turn—how many cards you draw, play, or discard

Think about: Shutting up and playing

Rather than discussing possible changes in the abstract, it is always better to grab an idea and just try it out. If the designers are not actually playing with some new rules within a minute or two, get them to zip their lips and playtest something.

Think about: One or two changes at a time

When tinkering with a system, if you change too much all at once, it's hard to know which change caused which effect. Encourage them to limit the number of changes they are trying out on a given playtest so that they have a better understanding of what's going on and why.

BALANCING SYSTEMS

TROUBLE IN DODGE CITY

Setup

Count 10 tokens for each player and put them in a single central pile

Shuffle the cards into a facedown deck

~~Deal a hand of 3 to each player;~~ keep your hand hidden

deal a hand of 5 to each player

Play

Oldest player goes first; take turns clockwise around the table

On your turn, draw a card and play a card; see chart below

Then discard the card you played unless another rule tells you to keep it

Play:	Action:
1 OUTLAW	*take 1 card randomly from any other player's hand* ~~Take 1 token from any other player~~
2 SALOON	Keep the saloon 2 out in front of you: for each saloon already out at the start of your turn, draw +1 card and play +1 card
3 MERCHANT	*you can play as many merchants as you want on a turn* ~~Take 3 tokens from the central pile~~
4 SHERIFF	Take 4 tokens from the central pile
5 MAYOR	*when you play a Mayor, discard another card* ~~Take 5 tokens from the central pile~~

End

The game is over immediately when there are no more tokens in the central pile

The player with the most tokens wins

4. Keep making changes

Once they have gone through a full round of iteration—making some changes, playing part or all of a game, and discussing what happened—*that's* when design really begins.

Let them reflect within each group. How did the last round of changes start to evolve the play of the game? Toward long-term strategic planning? Social alliances and devious backstabbing? Quicker and riskier play? For the next round of changes, do they want to accentuate the shifts that have started to happen, or do they want to push back and move the design in a different direction?

The goal is to get into an iterative loop—making changes, playtesting them, and discussing what happened—in order to make new changes. If they can repeat this cycle a few times, it'll be surprising how quickly a much better design will start to take shape.

Think about: Not finishing a game

Most of the time, the effects of a rules change can be felt in a turn or two. They shouldn't feel obligated to finish an entire game if they pick up on what's happening and want to make more changes. It's totally fine to scrap a game in progress, make new changes, and start playing again.

Think about: Better and worse cards are OK

It's counterintuitive, but it is often OK to have some game options that are simply better than others—for example, the Mayor (who gives you 5 tokens) is always better than the Sheriff (who gives you 4). You'll get that little thrill when you draw the Mayor card.

On the other hand, you probably need more than that to craft a meaningful choice. For example, perhaps you can play a pair of the same card for a bonus—you might have to agonize about whether to play a Mayor now or hold on to it and hope for another one to complete a set. Or maybe you've added opportunities to take cards from other players, in which case hanging on to good cards can become a liability.

5. Share designs with everyone

Depending on the available time, the groups may have barely managed to dip into a handful of changes, or perhaps they were able to go through many iterations and significantly redesign and balance the whole design. Both situations provide valuable experiences.

When you have 10 or 15 minutes left, shift to a discussion. The main learning of the exercise is the actual design and playtesting that happens within each group. That said, it's always helpful to have the groups share the changes that they made with each other.

Discuss: What did your group do with the design?

At this point, everyone is familiar with the way the game works, and you don't need to have groups actually play each other's designs. Each group can present a verbal summary of the changes they made, which should be enough for everyone to appreciate the work they did.

Discuss: Did the changes focus on special powers or on the core mechanics?

Many groups may have modified particular card abilities and effects—nerfing the Saloon or boosting the Merchant. Others might have changed the game economy, adjusting the deck composition or the amount of loot in the central pile. Still others may have changed what you do on your turn—perhaps you take 2 actions, or you play a card faceup, which sits vulnerable for a turn before the card power takes effect. None of these approaches are better or worse—it all comes down to the particular details and how they affected the play of the game.

Discuss: Were there any strange experiments?

Celebrate weird and unusual design ideas. Especially so-called failed experiments! Sometimes incremental changes can help you gradually approach a better balance. Other times, a more radical change can point you in a completely different and unexpected direction. Even when a proposed change is not fully successful, it can be very informative and lead to something more interesting than a balanced, but perhaps boring, game design.

Context

Trouble in Dodge City was designed specifically to explore dynamic feedback loops in games. It also works extremely well as a general exercise in redesigning a system. The starting game design is clearly broken but with many possible directions for improvement. Because it's a short game to play, the iteration cycle can quickly get off the ground. By the way, Trouble in Dodge City began life as Kingdom, a game set in a far-off medieval land. It could be rethemed again....That, of course, would be another exercise entirely.

BALANCING SYSTEMS

BOLF

BOLF is short
for Beanbag Golf.
Design BOLF "holes"
for others to play
while inventing
physical mechanics,
balancing enjoyment
and difficulty, and
practicing clear
communication.

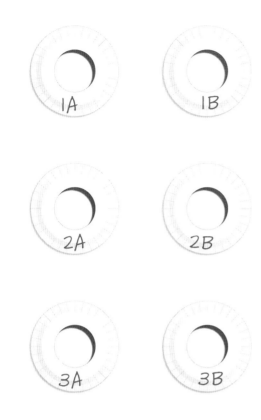

0. Preparation

The materials you'll need for running this exercise are:

- beanbags: ideally 1 per player, but minimum 1 per group
- paper plates: 2 per group
- thick markers, writing supplies, blank paper, a few rolls of masking tape
- game sheet, page 193, printed on card stock and cut: 1 card per designer

Groups of 3 or 4 participants works best. If you have 10 or fewer people involved, it's OK to have groups of 2.

For each group, you will need to create 2 paper-plate holes. Cut a circle out of the middle of a paper plate—about two-thirds of the plate's diameter—so that there is a very large hole in the center. These paper-plate rings will be the Golf-like holes into which people will try to toss the beanbags. They will be placed on the floor upside down so that the plate is like a little dome. If you have enough plates, it's probably better to stack a few together for each hole, just for structural integrity.

Use a marker to label the plates for each hole. Every group of designers will have a hole labeled A and another labeled B. For example, if you have 3 groups, there will be 6 paper-plate holes labeled 1A, 1B, 2A, 2B, 3A, and 3B.

What You Need

- 6 or more players in a large space
- 90–120 minutes
- Beanbags
- Paper plates
- Masking tape
- Paper and writing/drawing utensils
- Game sheet, page 193

What You Learn

- ◆ A physical approach to practicing level design
- ◆ Teaching players through design and communication
- ◆ The challenge of scaling difficulty for a particular audience

BALANCING SYSTEMS

BOLF

2. Give the design challenge

Now that they understand the basics, it's time to explain the real exercise: to design a unique pair of holes. Each group will be designing 2 holes—the first hole (A) is a tutorial hole, which teaches the basic idea to the player in a gentle way. The second hole (B) is an advanced hole, which builds on the concept of the tutorial hole but offers a deeper challenge. The starting Xs for the 2 holes can be the same spot or different spots (if they are different, they should be clearly labeled).

What kinds of challenges can the participants design? They can invent whatever physical structures and rule modifications they want, as long as the basic rules remain the same. Go through a quick verbal brainstorm to open up the possibilities. You might get answers like:

- *Golf-style hazards.* For example, sand traps (complete with stroke penalty), mapped out on the floor with masking tape

- *Spatial challenges.* Placing holes very far from the starting X, or requiring players to make a "skill shot," such as throwing a beanbag through a narrow opening as a requirement for finishing the hole

- *New rules.* A beanbag has to touch a series of checkpoints—maybe the checkpoints even "teleport" the beanbag to a new location

- *Physical challenges.* A player has to close their eyes or spin around before throwing, face a certain direction, or stand on one leg

Designers will create their holes with a target score of 7 in mind. Each pair of holes (A+B) aims to result in a total score of 7. It might be that a tutorial hole is designed to have 3 tosses, and the corresponding advanced version is designed for 4 tosses. Or perhaps 2 and 5. Or whatever combination makes sense for a given pair of holes.

1. Demonstrate BOLF

The first step is to show everyone how to play BOLF. The core of the game is incredibly simple. Pass out the BOLF cards to help them follow the basic rules:

- To set up, place an X on the ground with tape. This is the starting point. Put one of the paper-plate holes a good distance away, perhaps under a desk or around a corner.

- A player stands on top of the X and tries to toss a beanbag into the paper plate hole. Ideally, the hole will be in a tricky place, so they can't get it on the first try. After the beanbag lands on the ground, pick it up and stand on the spot where it landed. Then toss again.

- Count each toss as you go. You finish the hole when your beanbag lands completely inside the hole, touching the floor inside the paper-plate ring. Your score is the number of tosses you took. Just like in Golf, a low score is better.

Before they start to design, it's a good idea to walk them through common pitfalls in a design challenge like this one. You can structure the discussion by having them speculate about the possible failure points listed in the question below.

Discuss: Given what you know about the game, what do you want to avoid?

There are a number of common design mistakes that often happen in this exercise. See how many from the list below that the group can name, and feel free to bring up ones that they don't mention.

Forgetting to design through play. It's not enough to just discuss or even physically construct a hole if the team is not trying it out. Encourage them to design through an active process of just playing around with the beanbags and seeing what kinds of interactions are fun and interesting.

Making the tutorial too hard. The first hole should be as simple as possible—just barely enough to introduce the core idea. The advanced hole can elaborate on that idea and provide a more substantial challenge. Designers tend to underestimate how difficult it is to just learn a new concept, and tutorials are very often too complex. The tutorial hole they might think is boring is probably quite stimulating for someone playing it for the first time.

Not tuning difficulty for a new player. They need to balance the challenge so that the tutorial and advanced hole add up to 7 tosses for a first-time player. Designers tend to tune things for themselves, but they will play their own hole over and over as they design it. They are not a representative audience! The result is that almost everyone ends up designing holes that require more than 7 tosses to complete.

Not properly communicating the rules. Don't make the signage a last-minute task, or they won't have time to get it right. Make sure that they appreciate the challenge of communicating rules, and encourage them to use visuals, like diagrams, pictures, and maps, in addition to text. Small details, such as where the signage is placed and how it relates to the space overall, makes a big difference in how well it conveys information.

Think about: Teaching through design

The tutorial/advanced hole structure engages with the idea of educating your player. It is a very common technique to design a simple level or experience where players learn a new concept or way to play, followed by a more advanced one where that new knowledge is put to use. Video games use this principle in level design all the time.

Think about: Theme and variation

One of the challenges of interactive design is extending a core system through many reinventions. Leveraging a central theme through multiple variations can retain interest and provide new kinds of challenges and experiences. Can each group come up with a different approach for their hole that takes the gameplay in a new direction while still being true to the original rules and spirit of BOLF?

Think about: Communicating interaction

Each group will create signage to explain anything unusual about their hole. Starting and ending locations, as well as any special rules, should be clearly explained to players. Designers won't be present to explain their holes, so the holes and their signage need to be completely self-explanatory. Clear language and diagrams—perhaps a whole signage system— might be necessary to fully explain things.

BALANCING SYSTEMS

BOLF

Think about: Playtesting methodology

Even in this informal setting, there's a lot to learn about how to conduct a proper playtest. For example, if designers help out a confused playtester (instead of being silent), then what they are testing is their own ability to verbally explain the rules rather than how well their signage works to communicate their design.

3. Design a pair of BOLF holes

Off they go! Let each group find a location where they want to start constructing and playtesting their holes. Make sure each group ends up with a separate space that doesn't overlap with anyone else's.

Once they have had 5 or 10 minutes to get settled into their process, check in with each team. In the joyful chaos of prototyping physical play, they will most likely forget all about the common mistakes you just discussed with them. So keep an eye out and remind each group as needed. For example, make sure they are actively designing through play.

By the way, it's perfectly OK if they end up falling prey to the very pitfalls they identified—BOLFed on their own petards! The point of an exercise like this is not for everyone to do things perfectly but for the designers to experience making design mistakes themselves. Even if they know better.

4. Cross-group playtesting

The best way to give each team a dose of reality is to let them do some intergroup playtesting. About 10 or 15 minutes into designing, give them a 5-minute warning that their design time is about to end. When they are out of time, have each group send a representative to the next hole (e.g., someone from group 2 goes to visit hole number 3, someone from group 3 visits hole 4, someone from group 4 visits hole 1, etc.).

Let each group practice *observational playtesting*—have them be absolutely quiet and passively watch to see how the player interacts with the hole. (They will likely struggle with the instructions and take far more than 7 tosses to get the beanbag in.) Rotate an additional representative around to give each group another data point, and let them redesign. This process will add 15–20 minutes to the exercise, but it's well worth it if you have the time.

5. Big BOLF tournament

Have them finish their hole designs (for real this time). Usually, 30 minutes of total design time is enough. Gather everyone around and explain how the tournament is going to work. Each of the designers is going to wander around on their own and play other groups' holes. It isn't necessary for every designer to play every other hole, but try to play as many as possible. As they play, fill out a scorecard, noting the total score (A+B) for each hole. The maximum score you can get on a hole is 14 (double par). The individual winner is the player with the lowest average score, so they really should play to win! (And no, you cannot play your own hole in the tournament.)

Once the tournament starts, they cannot change anything about their holes. Designers will want to hover around their own hole to explain how it works. It's too late for all that! Shoo them away to play other people's holes.

The process of playing other holes may take a while—there can be bottlenecks around slower holes and shortages of available beanbags. (That's why it is not necessary for everyone to play every hole.) When you have about 15 minutes remaining, collect everyone for the wrap-up.

6. Scoring and final discussion

The scoring process can get complicated, but follow these steps and things should go smoothly:

- *Vote on special awards.* As indicated on the score sheet, each player votes for 2 special awards. You can't vote for your own hole.

- *Add up personal averages.* Everyone does a bit of math and averages their individual score. Write that down on the bottom of your score sheet.

- *Team averages.* On a whiteboard, or possibly on a shared online spreadsheet, make a column for each hole and let players put down their total (A+B) score in that column. Have them add an F (for most fun) or C (for most creative) next to their score if they are voting a special award for that hole (or make F and C columns if you are using a spreadsheet). Then each team averages the scores of their hole and adds up their special award votes.

Now determine the winners—find out who had the lowest average personal score and congratulate the individual winner. Being sensitive to not embarrass anyone, get a sense of everyone else's score too. There will probably be a big range. It's a good indication of the large variation in any random sampling—and there is definitely a lot of randomness in BOLF. Compare team scores to discover the 3 team awards: the most fun experience, the most creative design, and the most balanced hole (closest to an average score of 7).

BOLF!

Your name: Kim

Hole	Score (A+B)	Most Fun	Most Creative
1	8	☐	☐
2		☐	☐
3	5	☐	☑
4	7	☐	☐
5	14	☐	☐
6	12	☑	☐
7	9	☐	☐
8		☐	☐
9		☐	☐
10		☐	☐
11		☐	☐
12		☐	☐
13		☐	☐
14		☐	☐
15		☐	☐
16		☐	☐
Avg.	9.17		

Basic Rules

Stand on starting "X" and toss beanbag.

Stand where it landed and toss again.

Finish hole when beanbag touches ground inside hole.

Score is number of tosses.

Design a Hole

Make it a unique experience (you can add stroke penalties and special rules).

Design 2 holes:
- an easier tutorial hole "A"
- an advanced hole "B"

The stroke par for both holes must add to 7.

Create clear, self-explanatory instruction signs. (You will not be around when your hole is played!)

Tournament

Play as many holes as possible.

Fill out a scorecard for each hole you play by adding up your total score for A+B.

Max score for a hole is 14 (double par).

Vote for the most fun and most creative holes that you played.

Winning

Individual:
- the lowest average score

Teams:
- the hole with closest average to par 7, plus awards for most fun and creative

BALANCING SYSTEMS

Remote version: VOLF

BOLF can be translated into a remote video exercise: VOLF. (Which stands for Video-based BOLF, of course!) The main difference is that designers are working solo rather than in groups, and instead of a beanbag and a paper plate, they use a wadded-up piece of paper and a drinking cup.

Otherwise, the exercise can be run in the same way as BOLF:

- explain the basic mechanics
- have everyone work on their hole (with or without outside testing)
- have designers write their rules in a document and put it in a shared online folder
- and then run a tournament (a shared spreadsheet can help facilitate score calculation)

The VOLF game sheet on page 194 includes an outline of the exercise you can share with every participant, as well as a couple of sample holes (since it may be harder to visualize what a VOLF hole looks like through a video interface).

Context

BOLF is a delicious mix of physical play, human design, and difficulty tuning. At the NYU Game Center, BOLF is used to introduce a unit on video game level design. The kinds of design pitfalls that happen in BOLF and the design thinking to get out of them are widely applicable to digital games and many other kinds of dynamic complex systems. Initially inspired by Bernie DeKoven's Junkyard Golf, BOLF turns out to be very similar to an exercise by game designer Stone Librande that also involves tuning difficulty on a miniature golf–like game, but using ping-pong balls instead of beanbags.

Discuss: Why did certain holes get recognized?

Likely, the different awards (fun, creative, and balanced) were not given to the same holes. It could be that the most fun or creative hole was actually very easy—or very hard. What makes something fun or creative may very much depend on the surrounding context of the other holes. Or on audience taste. It's very subjective!

Discuss: Share your experience

What about someone else's BOLF hole was particularly compelling or intriguing? What was confusing or frustrating? Ask some of them to explain their votes for the most fun or most creative holes.

Discuss: Which holes found new variations on the core mechanic?

BOLF is a great demonstration of how a basic core mechanic (tossing a beanbag into a hole) can be extended in a huge variety of directions through space design and the addition of special rules. This happens in all kinds of fields, from furniture design to app development. Which variations were particularly elegant (did the most through the smallest changes)? Did any of the holes transform BOLF into something else entirely, without changing any of the core rules?

Discuss: Share your design process

What did they find surprising or unexpected about the process of designing BOLF holes? What did they learn from making use of an outside playtester? Was the group right about the kinds of mistakes that they were expecting to see?

An exercise in modular storytelling. Write a dozen pages on cards so that when you shuffle them and draw 5, you get a coherent story every single time.

A DECK OF STORIES

A DECK OF STORIES

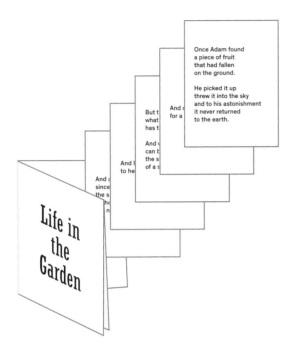

What You Need

- Any number of players, working in pairs
- 60–90 minutes
- Writing supplies
- Index cards (both standard and double-size)
- Game sheets, pages 195–197

What You Learn

- Techniques for interactive storytelling
- Designing at the intersection of systems and narrative
- Practicing modular story writing

0. Prepare for play

Print one copy of the Deck of Stories game sheets on card stock or paper to use for the demonstration. The first page is the "book cover"—cut out the square and fold as shown. The result is a miniature book that has "Life in the Garden" on the cover, "Adam, Eve, and the serpent lived in the garden" on the inside cover, and "The end" on the inside back cover. Print and cut game sheets on pages 196–197, to create a deck of 32 pages.

The designers will be creating their own books. They will need the following supplies (it's good to have some extras):

- about 15 blank standard-size index cards (3 × 5 in or a similar size) for every 2 designers
- 1 blank large index card (4 × 6 in, 5 × 8 in, or similar) for every 2 designers
- writing utensils

1. Demonstrate and discuss

Generate a story with the Life in the Garden demo deck of stories:

- First, shuffle the deck of pages;
- Then draw 5 pages at random, and place them between the covers;
- Finally, read the story out loud from beginning to end, including the cover and inside cover page, and concluding with "The end."

The randomized stories that come out of the deck are almost always surprisingly coherent fables. Rather than a pregenerated linear story, Life in the Garden is a narrative system that generates stories.

Discuss: What makes it work?

Ask the group what it is about the design and the writing that helps the stories find coherence. Keep a running list on a whiteboard. Possible answers might include:

A known backstory. The system assumes that the audience is generally familiar with the characters and story of the garden of Eden. Rather than having to start with a backstory, the experience leans on that existing knowledge to jump right into the narrative.

A small cast of characters. Eve, Adam, and the serpent come up on most of the cards—in fact, pairs of them appear on the same card sometimes. This repetition of characters within the narrative helps give the resulting story a sense of coherence.

A moment in time. All events take place in the ambiguous time after the creation of Eden but before the fall and the departure of Eve and Adam. Nothing happens that can contradict this or make any permanent changes. For example, none of the main characters actually die because if they then appeared on a later card, the plot would lose its logic.

Recurring themes and consistent mood. The pages all have a similar dreamlike tone and engage with themes like time, sleep, growth, and decay. This thematic and stylistic coherence helps the pages hang together and result in what feels like a single story.

Modular writing. The wording on each page is structured so that it can become the opening of the story or make for a satisfying ending. The writing needed for Life in the Garden is partly traditional storytelling and partly like designing Lego bricks. Each page is a modular unit of meaning that needs to be able to link up with what comes before and what comes after.

Implied causality. The "magic" of Life in the Garden happens when later pages seem to be responding to what already happened earlier. Part of this causality comes from tactical modular writing ("God was not pleased.") and part from strategic ambiguity. Our minds tend to fill in gaps so that events in a story make sense, as with graphic novels in which implied events can happen in the "gutters" between comic panels.

The tactile experience. Playing Life in the Garden feels like a sleight-of-hand magic trick—the shuffled pages somehow fall together into a logical shape. Would it work as a digital project, where a button click would produce a randomly generated story? Holding the entire deck in your hand keeps you in touch with the structure in a way that becomes hidden when it is all happening behind the curtain of a computer program. The physical component is an important part of the magic trick of the experience.

2. Generate scenarios

Enough discussion! It's time to design. In pairs, designers will be creating their own deck of stories—keeping the same structure as Life in the Garden but inventing their own content.

As a first step, brainstorm narrative scenarios that they might use. Keeping in mind the idea of a *known backstory*, write down possible story situations on a whiteboard as participants shout them out. For instance:

Myths and fairy tales:

- Theseus and the Minotaur
- Little Red Riding Hood
- Donald Trump's White House

Genre situations:

- Two cowpokes in a barroom brawl
- A vampire stalking a victim
- Survivors on a desert island

Shared cultural references:

- Harry Potter
- Romeo and Juliet
- A design workshop

Remind them that they're not telling the entire story—they'll need to find a *moment in time* that works for the limited scope of the book. For instance, a retelling of Little Red Riding Hood might focus just on the walk through the forest to Grandmother's house.

NARRATIVE SYSTEMS

A DECK OF STORIES

3. Design their own deck of stories

Divide the designers into pairs, and give each pair a stack of 15 index cards and one larger card. Each pair picks one of the brainstormed scenario ideas as the basis for their story. They'll be designing a book like Life in the Garden, with a deck of at least 12 pages.

The large card is used as the book cover—ask them to fold it in half, and remind them that they can use the front and back cover and the inside covers to set up and resolve their randomized story. Pass around the Life in the Garden demo if they want a closer look at the example story.

As they begin work, draw their attention to the list of brainstormed strategies, like a small cast of characters and modular writing, that make Life in the Garden work. They need to keep those in mind!

Think about: Rapid prototyping

Encourage them to design through iteration. Quickly make a set of 6 or 7 cards, and see which ones work and which don't work as well. Playtesting constantly and iterating on the pages is key. Have extra pages and covers on hand so they can revise as they go.

Think about: Whole from parts

The goal is that each time you play the deck of stories, the resulting narrative is more than the sum of the parts. Characters and events ideally generate relationships with each other so that the story feels like something unfolding through cause and effect. It's not too hard to come up with a series of plot points that makes logical sense—but can their stories leverage the semiotic magic of implied causality?

4. Share stories

About 30 minutes should be enough time for writing and design. When they are finished, have each group demonstrate another group's book by drawing a random story of 5 pages.

Talk about what is and isn't working in each one. It's hard to get everything right in such a short period of time! Likely, each book will have something interesting going on while suffering from other problems. For example, one book might have a very consistent tone but doesn't quite manage to achieve a web of causality.

Discuss: How did this kind of writing feel different than linear writing?

This exercise helps designers experience the strange constraints on writing that often happen in an interactive context. The structure of an interactive story will always put limits around language, plot, dialog, and other elements of a narrative.

Discuss: What makes particular pages work better than others?

Interactive stories are often wheels within wheels, and these decks of stories embody the way larger systemic elements and detailed language choices work together to result in an experience. The words on each individual page need to be compelling to a reader, and at the same time, the pages need to connect together into a larger story structure.

Discuss: What is the role of ambiguity in the experience?

The magic of an interactive story emerges from the interplay between clever design decisions and the audience's instinct to create meaning. Often a light touch can leave room for ambiguity that a reader is only too eager to fill in on their own.

For remote online play

In a remote situation: go solo. As long as everyone has access to writing utensils and index cards or paper, designers can create their own books and share them with each other by reading them out loud to the group. Because they are working solo, think about pairing them up for some quick playtesting and feedback halfway through the exercise.

Context

A Deck of Stories is a great exercise to introduce the strange territory at the intersection of systems design and narrative writing. It's good practice for interactive storytellers and is quite challenging, but can produce some terrific results. It is very relevant to the kinds of unpredictable narrative systems that digital designers often want to create. The exercise was inspired by the original *Life in the Garden* (1999) by artist and designer Nancy Nowacek and myself. It includes many more (and some very naughty) pages about the Garden of Eden characters, along with striking illustrations and design by Nancy.

Create a small town overrun by zombies. Playing the story through a tabletop game, find ways of systemically representing each of the town's quirky characters.

ZOMBIE TOWN

ZOMBIE TOWN

What You Need

- Any number of players, working in pairs
- 90–120 minutes
- 6-sided dice
- Small tokens to represent zombies
- Game sheets, pages 198–201

What You Learn

- ◆ Collaborative world-building techniques
- ◆ Procedural representation of characters in an interactive story
- ◆ How to shape narrative drama through emergent systems

0. Prepare for play

If this is your first time, play through a quick game by yourself so that you can better explain it to everyone else. The materials you'll need for running this exercise are:

- 1 copy of the character stands (game sheet page 198), printed on card stock
- the board (199), rules (200), and world sheet (201); 1 copy per pair of designers
- a 6-sided die for each pair of designers
- writing supplies
- small tokens to represent zombies (about a dozen per pair of designers)

Cut out the character stands. A digital or physical whiteboard is particularly handy for when everyone is brainstorming the characters and world together.

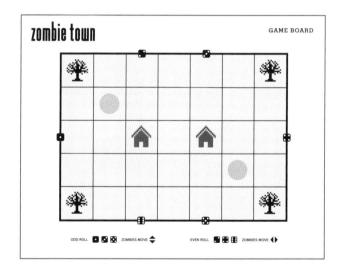

1. Build a world

Divide the group into pairs. Because the pairs will double up into larger groups later on, make sure to have an even number of groups. It's OK if 1 or 2 of the groups ends up with 3 people.

Give a world sheet to each pair. It's time for everyone to build out the setting and characters of Zombie Town together.

The setting. First, as a group, pick a name for the town where the zombie outbreak is taking place. Have everyone brainstorm 3 important facts about the town. For example: Inverwood, Indiana, is near an abandoned nuclear-waste site; there is a new mall in the middle of downtown; and the town government is known to be corrupt. Record the group decisions on the whiteboard, and they can take notes on their world sheet. Everyone will be using the same setting for the exercise, so everyone's town will be the same.

The characters. Next, sketch out some of the characters. Start by picking a character and give them a name that begins with the letter on the character sheet. Then add a short phrase that defines their core identity. Frankie, rebellious teen. Samuel, grizzled investigative journalist. Write each character name on the whiteboard along with any notes. You don't need to detail every character—you only need to define enough characters so that there will be one for each group (a few extras are OK too). All of the groups together will be using the same cast of characters, so as you define them, each pair of designers writes the same set of names and other information on their world sheet.

Character relationships. Now that you have sketched several characters, enrich their identities by drawing relationships between them. Are any of the characters romantic partners? Or family members? Or bitter rivals? Or some twisted combination? Brainstorm multiple relationships between different characters and take notes on the whiteboard, drawing connecting lines between characters and labeling the lines.

Think about: Working with and against genre

When quickly building a story world, the tendency is to lean heavily on genre. This can have advantages —genre characters can provide a familiar narrative shorthand. Genre also has its disadvantages— uncritically using stereotypes (for gender, race, age, etc.) can be very problematic. Encourage participants to invent characters who can break or contradict stereotypes and genre expectations.

Think about: Defining characters through relationships

It's remarkable how useful character relationships are for building story worlds. They really unlock creativity! Relationships suggest histories, desires, and hidden depths—they are a great tool for generating any kind of narrative setting.

Think about: World building from the bottom up

The process of brainstorming aspects of a town, then its characters and their relationships, offers participants a miniature experience of building an entire narrative world. Notice how the spirit of the setting emerges from the details of the world— the quirks of particular characters, their unexpected pairings and histories. This kind of distinctive texture is what makes a narrative setting memorable.

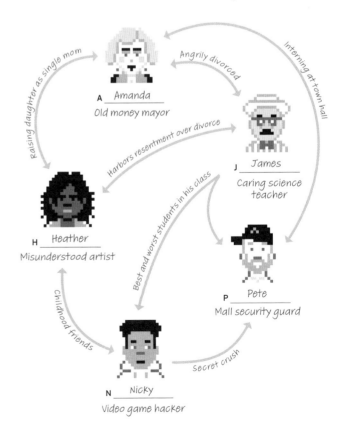

NARRATIVE SYSTEMS

2. Pick a character and play the basic game

Pass out one board and rules page to each pair of designers, along with a 6-sided die. Each pair gets to select one of the previously defined characters and takes the relevant cut-out character stand back to their table. There is only one stand for each character, so each group will end up with someone different.

First, everyone places their character on one of the gray spots on the board and puts a token on the number 3 on the bottom of the rules page to keep track of the character's health. Then walk them through the turn sequence, step by step. For this first game, none of the characters will have special actions, and the players will only be able move to an adjacent square in step 2. Since there is just one character on the board, there is nothing to do (yet!) in step 4.

As they play through a game, more and more zombies will appear on the edges and shuffle toward the character, who can dodge them at first but will eventually be surrounded and perish when their health reaches 0. Noooo!

Think about: An inevitable ending

Zombie Town is not meant to be a winnable game. It's fairly guaranteed that the characters will die. Tragedy is powerful, and not all stories have to be power fantasies about overcoming impossible odds. There is a special kind of grim drama in the inevitable.

Think about: A ticking clock

The pacing of Zombie Town is determined by the steadily increasing zombies on the board and the steadily decreasing health of the characters in the scene. The pace begins slowly—it's initially easy to avoid just a handful of zombies—but accelerates as more zombies lead to more chances for a character to be surrounded and lose health points. Anything that accelerates these factors (more zombies, faster zombies, lower character health) will speed the ticking clock; anything that pushes back against them will slow down the pace of the game.

Example:
A few turns into the game, the player rolls a 🎲 and a zombie token is placed at the 🎲 marker

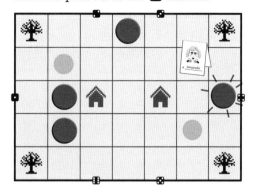

The player decides to move one space to the left

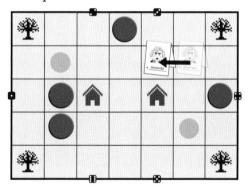

Because it was an even roll, all zombies move **horizontally** toward the player if they can

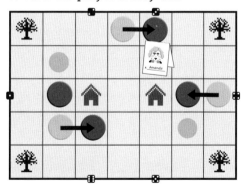

One zombie ended this turn next to the player, so the player's health is reduced by 1 on the character sheet

zombie town

SETUP

Place your character(s) on a gray spot on the board

Put a token marker on the 3 below to keep track of health

PLAY

Each turn, go through the following steps in order:

1. Place a new zombie

Roll a die and place a new zombie in that space if it is empty

(If the space is not empty, don't place a new zombie this turn)

2. One character moves

Move any character into an adjacent empty space — or — do any special action

A space with a tree, house, or other character is NOT empty; characters cannot move there!

3. All zombies move

Move each zombie one space toward the character that just moved or took an action:

- if the roll was even, move horizontally ◀▶
- if the roll was odd, move vertically ▲▼

Zombies can only move into empty spaces but will wait for each other to move out of their way if they can

A space with a tree, house, or other character is NOT empty; zombies cannot move there!

It is possible that a Zombie will not move at all if it is already "lined up" with a character

4. Other character moves

If there is another character, move into an adjacent empty space — or — do any special action

5. Zombies attack!

A character loses 1 Health for each zombie in a directly adjacent space

If a character's Health goes to zero, the character is eliminated

If all characters die, the zombies win

YOUR CHARACTER

zombie town

Name: Heather, misunderstood artist

What drives this character:
Desire to escape this small town; Intuitive connection with nature

HEALTH (0) (1) (2) (**3**)

SPECIAL ACTIONS

Solo movement action:
Heather can climb into a tree space. Adjacent zombies still damage her

Another solo action (something that isn't just movement):
When Heather is in a tree, she can use an action to dream of escape and increase her health by 1.

Character combo action (involves another character):

NARRATIVE SYSTEMS

3. Design the character

Now that the participants have a sense for how the game works, it's time for each group to flesh out their selected character. Every pair fills out the character sheet at the bottom of the rules page with the following information:

What drives the character? Given the character's identity and relationships, what is the emotional or psychological core of the character? How would they respond to a dangerous and uncertain situation, like being in a town overrun by zombies? Are they driven by a scientific impulse to uncover the truth? Or a long-repressed anger at their abusive boss? Write a summary of the character's internal drive on the sheet.

Solo movement action. Design a movement-oriented action that the character can optionally take instead of the default movement (moving one space to an adjacent square). Perhaps the character can move diagonally, or jump an extra space, or hide in one of the houses on the board. It's OK to add some special rules, such as only being able to use the special action once per game.

Another solo action (something that isn't just movement). Finally, design a second special action that isn't just about their movement. Perhaps they can heal a point of health or freeze a zombie on the board. Or even spill something on the ground that keeps the zombies away (you can use a different kind of token to keep track of the spill on the board). Again, it's perfectly fine to invent special conditions and effects, as long as they don't get too elaborate or complicated.

The 2 new actions are both solo actions, involving just the single character and nobody else. (Leave the bottom "Character combo action" blank for now.) The design challenge here is to invent 2 possible actions that express the character's persona through the system of the game.

Think about: Procedural representation

One of the ways that interactive systems can depict stories and content is through rules and procedures. The Knight on a chessboard doesn't just look like a mounted soldier, it can actually leap over other pieces because of the rules that define its identity. Making systems narratively expressive is an important kind of design thinking.

Think about: Avoiding power gaming

Remind everyone that their goal is not to invent abilities that will help the character defeat the zombies. It's easy enough to come up with superpowers that will clear the board of enemies! The deeper questions are: Do the powers feel right for the character? Do they express the personality and spirit of the character? Help the designers embrace the tragic, almost-certain death of their beloved character.

Once their powers are designed, have them play through a full game and try them out. When they reach step 2 of the turn sequence ("One Character Moves"), instead of the normal movement action, their character can optionally use one of their 2 special actions.

After the playtest, the designers are free to tweak the character abilities. Remember, the goal is to design the actions so that they genuinely depict the character's core identity.

4. Pair up characters

The final design challenge will expand the scene to include 2 characters. Take a look at the whiteboard and the relationships between the characters that everyone brainstormed. Discuss which characters selected by groups should be paired up in a scene together. It might turn out that a couple of characters end up together that don't yet have a defined relationship—that's OK!

Double up the groups based on the 2 characters who will be together in a scene. That means there will now be groups of 4 designers, made up of the 2 pairs of designers who have been working on the 2 characters in the scene. Have each group go through the following steps:

- *Introduce themselves.* Each group shares the information on their character sheet—the character drive as well as both of the special actions.

- *Discuss the relationship.* Make sure that everyone has a common understanding of the relationship between the 2 characters. This may involve inventing or deepening the history between them.

- *Invent character-combo actions.* Design new special actions for each of the 2 characters. The action is based on the relationship between them and involves both characters. For example, the action can take effect only when the 2 characters are next to each other, or when one is injured or surrounded by 2 or more zombies. The 2 characters should each get different actions that express their individual personality and how they feel about the other character.

YOUR CHARACTER

zombie town

Name: Heather, misunderstood artist

What drives this character:
Desire to escape this small town; Intuitive connection with nature

HEALTH (0) (1) (2) (**3**)

SPECIAL ACTIONS

Solo movement action:
Heather can climb into a tree space. Adjacent zombies still damage her

Another solo action (something that isn't just movement):
When Heather is in a tree, she can use an action to dream of escape and increase her health by 1.

Character combo action (involves another character):
When Heather and Nicky are in adjacent spaces, Heather gains the courage from their childhood friendship to push an adjacent zombie away from her one space.

NARRATIVE SYSTEMS

ZOMBIE TOWN

There will be a lot to discuss. Remember— the goal is not to invent superpowers! This is a storytelling exercise. The combo actions should express the narrative relationship between the 2 characters.

Try to get them playing quickly. Each group sets up their scene and plays it through. The game plays the same, with these adjustments for the 2-character scene:

- *Place both characters on the board.* At the start of the game, put the stands for the 2 characters on the 2 gray spots on the board.

- *Each character takes 1 action per turn.* When you reach step 2, decide which character will take their action—that character can do a normal movement action, 1 of the solo actions, or the combo action.

- *Zombies move toward the character who did something.* In step 3, the zombies will always move toward the character who just took an action in step 2. So it can be important to decide who distracts the shambling zombies on a given turn.

- *The other character takes an action after that.* The character who didn't take an action in step 2 will take their action in step 4. Which character moves first can vary from turn to turn.

Then let them play. These scenes will take longer to play through, as there are more decisions to make and more options each turn. There might be some fussy rules complications for groups to figure out, but that's OK. As they play, things might start to get intense. It's a good sign when you hear players shrieking out in the voice of their characters. If a group finishes early, have them play another game.

5. Share stories

A great way to wrap up this exercise is simply to have groups share the story of what happened in their 2-character scene. You are likely to hear thrilling tales of harrowing near-death experiences, as well as tragic moments in which loved ones sacrificed themselves to the oncoming zombie horde.

Discuss: What unexpected drama emerged? What role did the design play?

One remarkable thing about Zombie Town is that emotionally intense narratives can bubble up out of a fairly abstract system. The simple mechanics of Zombie Town becomes a kind of platform for telling a range of stories about a whole cast of characters.

Discuss: What is immersion and how does it happen in a game like Zombie Town?

So-called immersion does not have to be about photorealistic graphics and fancy visual effects. It is more often about emotional, psychological, and social engagement. In Zombie Town, the experience of co-creating a world and the growing fluency with the system help players see past the die rolls and cardboard pieces to become incredibly invested in the stories.

Context

In video games and other interactive narratives, there often is an impulse to express stories and character not only through dialog and visuals but also through interaction and logic. I find that Zombie Town efficiently brings together the simultaneous challenges of systems design and storytelling to practice exactly this kind of design thinking. Plus it gives everyone the experience of coming up with a compelling cast of characters in a very short period of time, demystifying the sometimes intimidating notion of world building. Zombie Town is based directly on a wonderful design exercise by Stone Librande called 100 Zombies that also explores procedural representation and emergent drama—also by way of the undead.

DESIGN

He didn't want to get lost in the woods. So he made
a very small forest, with just one tree in it.

Crockett Johnson
Harold and the Purple Crayon

A FEW WAYS TO THINK ABOUT DESIGN

MORE THAN ONE ANSWER

Designers are pragmatists. The value of a design concept is its utility in solving a problem. Be flexible and switch between ways of thinking when you need to.

How does a game affect people? What makes a game popular? What is the function of games in culture? These kinds of questions come up a lot—and in every field, not just in games. How does a *building* impact people? What makes a *book* popular? What is the function of *images* in culture?

Questions like these seem reasonable on first glance, but they are a trap. The problem is the assumption that there's one single answer, a simple truth behind a complex cultural phenomenon. What is the function of images in culture? Well, it all depends. Which image, for whom, in what kind of context? An abstract painting? An advertising billboard? Internet porn?

It is exactly the same with games. Imagine tossing a ball with a puppy, winning a beauty contest, or backstabbing your friends in *Among Us* (2018)—the forms and functions and meanings of games are radically varied. Games are not one thing, they are many things. There is no single right answer to questions about what they are and how they work. The challenge is being able to choose the answer that meets your needs as you wrestle with a particular design problem.

For example, say that players are not able to level up quickly enough to beat a final boss. This sounds like a problem you can tackle if you think of a game as a system of positive and negative

feedback loops. That formal understanding can help you shift some stats and tweak a difficulty curve so that players are able to get to the end of the game properly buffed to win.

At another moment in designing the same game, a different problem could emerge: none of the players are connecting with the game's protagonist. Heck, they're not even remembering her name! Solving this kind of problem requires a new understanding of how games work, such as the idea that a game involves a layering of person, player, and character. To connect players to the main character, you might need to rethink her narrative persona or work to shift the cultural expectations of the audience.

So which is true? Are games formal systems? Cultural spaces? Something else? The answer is yes. For a designer, value comes from utility. A concept is important or meaningful because it helps you solve a particular problem at a particular moment during a process. Contrasting ideas aren't contradictions. They are just different bat-tools on your utility belt of useful concepts.

We all want to understand what it is that we're designing. But be skeptical of simple answers to complex questions: the grand unifying aesthetic theory, the uncomfortably narrow definition, or the one-size-fits-all creative process. The reality is that sometimes we are solving mathematical problems and sometimes problems of dramatic pacing. Or social psychology, or political engineering. Train yourself to be flexible.

Of course this isn't the case just for games but for anything you are making. You are empowered to decide what is more or less useful or true for you, right now, as you design. Even if tomorrow it becomes something else entirely.

A PROCESS OF SOLVING PROBLEMS

Design is the process of learning how to solve problems. That process itself needs to be intentionally designed— if you get the process right, the solution will take care of itself.

"Where do you get your ideas?" This is a question an artist or designer or other creative person is often asked when they talk about what they do. Too often. The question implies that the most important moment in the life cycle of a project is the moment of conception, the mythical instant of genius when the answer appears in the creator's mind, and that the rest of the work after that is just fleshing out the details. There's just one problem: that story is dead opposite of reality.

Why? Because it ignores what is actually far more important: the process. An initial idea is just a starting point. The hard work, the real work, the place of discovery and creativity, is each step along the way. I'm not the first to say it: ideas are cheap. Everyone has good ideas. Just about any starting point can lead somewhere interesting. The real question is: How are you going to get there?

In an episode of the series *Abstract* (2019), the toy designer Cas Holman is designing a new kind of playground, but she's dissatisfied with her sketches. Her doodles of gym bars, slides, and climbable objects are too focused on the objects themselves and not on what kids can actually do with them. So she changes her process: she starts drawing kids in very unusual positions— in wild, gymnastic poses. Only then does Holman try to figure out what kind of playground

equipment designs could possibly get their bodies to make those strange gestures. She tricks her own brain into taking on a new creative process.

There is no official handbook of playground design that told her what to do. Holman did what every designer does: invent a process that would help her solve the problem. Here's a working definition of design: *design is the process of learning how to solve problems*. Designing something is like crossing a river. To get to the opposite bank, you'll need to put down some stepping-stones. As you design, you place one stone after another—with every step forward, you can get new perspective, reassess what you already did, and plan your next move. Focus on each step, one by one, and eventually you'll get there.

The process extends beyond just prototyping and playtesting. How do you define roles and responsibilities? How does the physical layout of a workspace facilitate productive interaction? How are important creative decisions made? To answer these hard questions, you need to apply design thinking to the structure of your collaboration. The hierarchies, policies, and processes of a company or a team are like the rules of a game. The play that happens—the interactions, the experiences, the unexpected creativity—emerges from the designed frameworks that give rise to it. The final products are really nothing more than the residue of that designed process.

In other words, the design process is itself a design problem, one that needs careful thought and iteration. In a well-designed process, just like in a game, there is a balance between structure and freedom, between planning and improvisation. From among and between the rules, unexpected play bubbles up. Creative play that can surprise your best-laid expectations. And hopefully result in something much better than whatever that first idea ever was.

SHARED AUTHORSHIP

In a healthy collaboration, each person has the autonomy to make creative decisions. Paradoxically, clearly defining everyone's roles allows people to move beyond them.

The hardest part of making something collaboratively is not actually making it. It's getting everyone to work together smoothly. If everyone involved in a project can pull together, you can move forward through the problems that inevitably come up without getting stuck.

People put their full creative energies into a project when they feel ownership of a project. When they're not just clocking in, doing some tasks, and clocking out. When it is truly their own work. How do people get a genuine sense of real authorship over what they do? The answer is brilliantly simple: don't fake it. They need to have actual, real authorship. The only way to make someone feel like they are making important decisions is to let them make important decisions. This is the opposite of a more traditional approach, in which a lead designer or creative director carries the vision for a project and has final approval over everything. Giving everyone on a team autonomy sounds scary, and it is! Yet it's the only way to really get everyone's heads in the game.

So how does this not devolve into anarchy? The first step is to clearly define everyone's roles and responsibilities—and to give them actual autonomy within that clearly defined role.

If Andrea is composing the music for the game, Andrea is responsible for what it sounds like. Andrea makes the decisions. But Andrea doesn't just work in isolation. Every person is bound to the team through copious amounts of *respect*, *trust*, and *communication*. There needs to be mutual respect and creative trust that everyone is competent in what they need to do—and constant communication so that everyone's individual work is continually integrated.

Without respect, trust, and communication, autonomy becomes territorial: *Don't tell me what music to put in, that's my job!* But with respect, trust, and communication from all sides, something magical happens. People become enthusiastic for feedback and input. Autonomy becomes responsibility: each person's work integrates with what everyone else is doing. You know something extraordinary is happening when everyone is generating and sharing ideas beyond their official duties—the composer has story notes, the writer is tweaking the interface, the programmer is brainstorming level designs. Surprisingly, clarifying roles helps people traverse and transgress those very boundaries.

Shared authorship is very hard to get right. It's possible to crank out projects—even really interesting ones—by way of a bad process. The problem is that the team will want to kill each other by the time they reach the finish line. The best way to maintain happy collaborators with productive, sustainable working relationships is for everyone to feel that they are responsible for what they are doing. That in the end, their work is their work.

To truly embed shared authorship in an organizational culture means designing not only the creative process but also the organization itself. Here's a design challenge: Can you redesign revenue models, intellectual property agreements, and structures of corporate ownership to reflect the values of shared authorship?

EMBRACE PLAYTESTING

Playtesting is fundamental to iterative design. Know why you're playtesting. Learn to observe closely. Collaborate with your audience.

Prototype, playtest, redesign. Then repeat. The practice of making something by trying out an early version of it is at the heart of iterative design. Playtesting goes by many names: editing, rehearsal, modeling. It is a methodology that can be applied to just about any field and any kind of project.

Question: When do you start playtesting? Answer: Before you think you are ready. If you feel totally comfortable sharing your work in progress, it's probably too late! Playtest as early as you can so that there is still time to make changes based on any findings you discover. It's worth the effort: an afternoon of early playtesting might save six months of misplaced production time. Being able to start before you are ready requires strategic planning. Can you scale down a massively multiplayer experience to a dozen participants in a room? Can you prototype a complex digital interface as a paper-based puppet show?

In *A Primer for Playtesting* (2016), architect Nathalie Pozzi and I break the process down into 3 parts: considerations before, during, and after a playtest. Before a playtest, *set an intention*. The most important thing is to know why you are playtesting—the question or questions you hope the playtest will answer. Plan your methodology around those questions. There will be unexpected things you discover, but know why you want to hold the playtest in the first place.

During a playtest, *shut up and watch*. Observational playtesting—watching someone struggle and misunderstand—is incredibly hard. Still, it is a thousand times more useful than what we all have a tendency to do: to jump in and tell our testers what to do. If you explain things, you are only testing your ability to explain, not the design itself. If they ask a question, answer it with a question. (Q: What does the red button do? A: What do you think it does?) Encourage them to think aloud—perhaps two people talk through a single-player experience. All the while, keep your eyes and ears open and take detailed notes. Avoid what game designer Frank Lantz calls "happy face syndrome," paying too much attention to the successful moments. Instead, hunger for failure and relish in the breakdowns and struggles—because that's how your design improves.

After a playtest, *dialog*. Ask questions, get information, collect data. Collaborate with your playtesters. They may very well have concrete suggestions for improvement. You don't have to implement their ideas—remember that they are the patient and you are the doctor. The priority is not *what* they suggest but *why*. Your playtesters can do something you cannot—see your design with fresh eyes. Value that gift they bring to you.

Design the process. Be intentional. Be open to the unexpected. Playtesting will expand your sense of self to include teammates, colleagues, and strangers. It is soul-enriching to overcome your fear, let others tinker with your horribly broken prototype, and realize that they have valuable feedback that can help you learn and grow. So that you can playtest again.

CREATIVITY= LITERACY+FREEDOM

Creativity means breaking rules and playing with structures. It requires deep literacy of what already exists but also the freedom to step past it into strange new spaces.

Creativity comes up a lot these days. Creative ideas, creative solutions, creative ways to work and to live. There is often a cultlike reverence that crops up around creativity that can feel creepy. At the same time, there's no doubt that innovative thinking is important. Complex problems—of social inequity, of cultural understanding, of environmental collapse—require creative thinking and creative solutions.

Like a game, creativity is about playing with a system—questioning, bending, and breaking rules, freeing yourself from established thinking, and overthrowing convention. To break rules requires knowing what the rules are and giving yourself permission to leave them behind. This approach to creativity comes down to two things: having literacy about what already exists and feeling the freedom to go beyond it.

Literacy: a rigorous understanding of the domain in which you want to be creative. Why is this important? Having a sense of what is already out there prevents you from burning out your creative energy reinventing the wheel. If you want to shake up interactive storytelling, spend some time with the classics: Choose Your Own Adventures and Dungeons and Dragons. Also, dig into the latest hotness: immersive theater, walking simulators, AI-based interactive fiction. This doesn't have to be scholarly research—it should be fun! Dive in and experience what others have already done. Discover the rules that they follow and the ones that they break.

Freedom: giving yourself permission to play. In addition to literacy, creativity requires the freedom to fail, to have bad ideas, to be goofy, to bark up the wrong trees, to not really know where you are going and what you are doing. More than anything else, freedom is a feeling that happens in your body, in interactions with others, and in your thought process. If you are running a brainstorm and see people sitting rigid in their seats, try to help them unblock their minds and access a sense of freedom by getting their bodies moving. Many of the play exercises in this book are specifically geared to get everyone feeling loose and free, physically and mentally.

For a great example of hardcore creativity, consider Chindōgu, the "art of useless inventions." It has produced such absurd objects as foot umbrellas to keep shoes dry and a chopsticks-mounted fan for cooling down hot soup noodles. In fact the now-ubiquitous selfie stick first appeared as a Chindōgu invention in the 1990s— twenty years before it caught on! Kenji Kawakami invented Chindōgu and its philosophy, embodied in ten principles, including: *Chindōgu are tools for everyday life*; *Chindōgu are not for sale*; *Inherent in every Chindōgu is the spirit of anarchy*. Chindōgu means embracing these sometimes contradictory, rule-breaking rules.

Chindōgu reminds us that radical weirdness and rigorous thinking are not opposites but that they go hand in hand. Creativity emerges through a process that is sometimes intuitive and sometimes intentional. Literacy maps a field, highlighting the conventions that you want to break—which then can happen if you give yourself the freedom to do so. Creativity is a cycle of wild play alternating with careful assessment; each project and each person finds their own rhythm.

Creativity happens when structures— collaborative teams, school classrooms, city neighborhoods, decision-making processes—are designed for it. It's time to rethink the design of policies and organizations to facilitate more rigorous literacy and more radical freedom.

A CULTURE OF CRITIQUE

Giving and receiving feedback is an essential part of the design process. Fostering an environment of thoughtful, supportive critique helps everyone improve.

In social media, there's a very particular model for what critique looks like. In a contentious Twitter exchange or an argumentative Facebook thread, people try to argue against, shout down, or just out-and-out dismiss whatever point of view is being critiqued. But nothing could be further from a good design critique.

The goal of a design critique is not to be *right* but to be *helpful*. Critique connects the dots: What is this person trying to do? What have they actually done so far? How can you help them cross the space between those two points? Giving and getting good design critique is difficult—but it is absolutely essential.

Wherever you run these exercises, it should be a priority to establish a healthy culture of critique, a context in which all participants are comfortable offering and receiving critical feedback. Set this expectation by being very explicit about it—tell everyone that being comfortable with critique is a key part of why they are there. Thoughtful, supportive criticism is the highest form of respect that one designer can show to another designer.

Criticism is not just for the person receiving the criticism. It is also for the person giving it and for everyone else present. To give meaningful feedback, you need to put yourself inside someone else's project, understand what is going on, and then strategize about how to communicate your feedback in a useful way. It's exhausting! Giving multiple crits back to back is like running mental sprints. It will seriously sharpen your thinking and make you a better designer.

A few things to avoid. First, offering polite noncomments ("it's interesting") or no comments at all. If thoughtful criticism is the highest form of respect, it's important to show respect by actually saying something meaningful. Silence is disrespectful! Next, stay away from aggressive feedback. Some schools of thought view a design crit as a kind of character-building exercise in humiliation. That approach is not helpful—it's actually an abuse of power. A critique should help someone grow, not leave emotional scars.

Last, it may seem counterintuitive, but stay away from the other extreme—overly supportive feedback. Criticism is not unconditional love. It is called criticism for a reason—it is important to actually be critical. Resist the urge to say only good things to buffer against the anxiety of presenting vulnerable, half-finished work. Always be sensitive to how your comments will impact others, but in the end only the hard truth will set them free.

Criticism is like spicy food. It is painful at first, but then you develop a taste for it. Eventually, you can't get enough. The goal is to inculcate that craving to give and receive feedback—hard-hitting, helpful, sensitive, insightful feedback—in yourself and your collaborators.

To give thoughtful design critique is intrinsically humanizing. You adopt another's point of view, putting your own sensibility aside to help someone else realize theirs. There's a subtle art to giving a brutally rigorous critique that is also kind and caring. It's something that we can't ever practice enough.

EDUCATING AN AUDIENCE

Before they can interact with it, an audience needs to learn the system you are designing. Teaching them how to interact with a design should be part of the process from the start.

Every designer is also an educator. When you make a space, an object, or a situation, you want others to explore, inhabit, and play with it. Eventually, the audience may even become experts or virtuosos of your design. But before any of that can happen, they need to learn the basics.

A design is like a language. The audience needs to figure out how to how to speak and understand it. A design needs to lead them gently and patiently, while the unfamiliar gradually becomes familiar. The more strange and unusual your design, the more challenging it will be to teach.

In tabletop games, written rules are the traditional way that a designer teaches others how to play. Of course, most people learn games by playing with friends who have played before or by watching a video online. But the written rules still need to be impeccably put together. They are the educational "safety net"—if the rules don't make sense, the online streamer or early adopter isn't going to understand how to play in the first place.

Unlike video games, the "software" for board and card games—the rules themselves—run in the minds of the players. Their brains are the CPU! Making a complex system intuitive and clear enough to be quickly and easily understood is a tremendous design challenge. This is why making physical games provides such incredible practice in communicating to and teaching an audience.

Written tabletop instructions have two main roles. They are a *tutorial*—they need to teach new players how to play. They also are a *reference* —they are what experienced players consult to resolve questions and disputes. This makes them very tricky to write. Which concept needs to come before which? Do you aim for scannable brevity or robust redundancy? How can you deploy image and word, diagram and flowchart, flavor and style, to communicate the system?

Digital systems like video games have a different set of challenges. The best video game tutorials teach players effortlessly, giving them just-in-time information, integrating learning seamlessly into gameplay, adding new and more complicated elements right when players are ready for them. Video game players have been spoiled by detailed digital tutorials: they love to hate them, even as they desperately need them to learn how to play.

Whether it's on a tabletop, a screen, or anyplace else, start designing the learning experience as soon as possible. Never save it until the very end. Fake it as you make it: perhaps you read an audio tutorial out loud as they playtest your early prototype, or you mock up a tutorial animation on paper as a comic-book storyboard. Teaching an audience—figuring out how to best introduce new concepts into their heads—needs to be a part of every design problem. It's only after learning the basics of your design that they will start to do all of the amazing things that you want them to do—even things you never thought of.

Teaching through design improves your design—and your humanity too. As you learn to teach someone else, you discover the world through their eyes. That's something everyone can benefit from.

COMMUNICATING IS DESIGNING

Communicating an idea does not mean just conveying a preexisting concept. In figuring out how to articulate an idea, you design and evolve that idea.

Design is at least 50 percent communication. Designers communicate with collaborators throughout the process. They communicate with clients, publishers, and bosses to get a green light and keep going. Designers communicate constantly with their audiences, too, through interfaces, logos, stories, spaces. Every time someone acts and an interactive system responds, that response needs to be communicated. If a player is not aware that the tree fell down in the virtual forest, it doesn't matter if it really fell or not.

I used to think that designers first think up ideas and then afterward convey those ideas to someone else. That's completely backward. What I have come to understand is that the act of communication is itself an opportunity for design thinking. Figuring out how to articulate an idea to teammates, to funders, to players— this is how the idea takes shape. Visualizing a system or writing out user instructions is not documenting something that already exists— that act of communication is design work.

For instance, when first writing out the rules for a game, think about how those rules will impact the audience. What terminology, what layout, what style of writing makes the most sense? You can't design a chair without thinking of a human body. You shouldn't communicate a design without considering how someone's mind will inhabit the space of meaning you are crafting.

Communication is an opportunity to learn about how people think. In the video game industry, game designer Stone Librande has popularized the idea of one-page design documents, which explain a complex system through a single visualization. It originated from Librande's frustration, as the game designer on a large team, writing traditional "design bibles" hundreds of pages long that no one ever read. One day, he noticed that a programmer had printed out a game's level schematic and taped it on the wall. Librande realized that this kind of communication—visual, efficient, focused, digestible—could work much better. He shifted away from text-heavy design docs to posterlike visualizations in the form of maps, flowcharts, wireframes, and storyboards.

Communication is also about understanding both sides of the equation—not only the ideas being communicated but also the context in which they will be received. Librande's one-page design documents are not beautiful posters meant to immortalize a design—although they often are very stunning! They are the opposite: ephemera meant to be marked up, modified, redesigned, and replaced.

A complex project is always a moving target as a design changes and evolves through iteration. Communication not only records these changes but drives them forward. Learning to communicate—verbally sharing ideas, leveraging word and image, visualizing complex systems —is a way of training design. Each moment of communication is a chance to more deeply understand how you think, how others think, and how we can better understand each other.

DISOBEY THE RULES

There are no universal rules of good design. Any concept about how design works is merely a starting place for improvisation. Breaking rules is how things evolve.

This book is not short on strident advice: how to think about play; how to understand design; how to structure a collaboration. Don't let the enthusiasm fool you. There are no rules of good design. The ideas in here are not laws chiseled in stone. They are propositions meant to be questioned, broken down, and refashioned into something new.

When we study and practice something, there is a tendency to overemphasize the proper way of doing it. When I have trained in martial arts, techniques are taught with precision: this stance puts 60 percent of the weight on the front leg; the back foot is at a 45 percent angle. In reality, when you're in an actual fight, you're never going to ask your opponent to pause a moment while you pull out a protractor and measure the angle of your instep. You'll be using the techniques you were taught in a messy, chaotic, catch-as-catch-can improvisation.

When wrestling a challenging design problem, you'll never use a "rule" of good design in a pristine, orthodox way. As you make your way through a project, you'll be doing whatever you can, however you can. Being a designer means having the cognitive flexibility to flow between multiple roles: sometimes you're a number-crunching gearhead or a gregarious party host, other times a spellbinding storyteller or a political provocateur.

Games are not one thing; they are many things. This means that any rule of good design can be discarded at any moment, if necessary. Take something that seems undeniably fundamental: the uncertainty of how a game will end. If you already know who is going to win or lose, why play in the first place? Keeping players in suspense about the ending seems like a universal rule of good game design. Is it, though? Maybe it could present an interesting design challenge: make a game where the player is always going to lose, but they still want to play anyway. Or perhaps the game makes them forget about winning and losing altogether. The point is that there isn't a single rule of designing a game that can't be broken. That's how design and art grow and change—by overthrowing what came before.

What about something that seems even more foundational, like the concept of iterative design? This book is based on the idea of designing through prototyping and play, yet that doesn't mean it's always right. Revising and balancing too much can ruin the wildness and quirkiness of a design. Designer and artist mattie has written about the limitations of iterative design: that not all games need to be centered on the needs of the player, that relying on playtesting can mean you are watering down critical ideas to placate an audience, or that it can make you complicit in the capitalist drive to build efficient machines that min-max pleasure for profit. So down with iterative design!

There simply are no universal rules of good design. Rules mark out a territory. You might go down the path they indicate, just the way it was intended, or you might parkour through in your own unique fashion. You can turn your back on those design rules and head in a completely different direction. Or maybe you stick around just long enough to tear down the whole darn thing.

LEARN TO LISTEN

Design is a way of practicing human sensitivity. Learn to listen to playtesters— it will expand your sense of authorship to include others.

Design puts us in touch with other human beings because design means designing something for someone else to experience. A key part of the process is learning to listen to others, to become attuned to the way people think, respond, and interact. Designing for someone else isn't just about identifying a target audience for a final product. It's also about observing your audience and opening yourself up to what they have to say. As you prototype and playtest and tune in to your audience, they become your collaborators.

Many years ago, a friend who was working as an auto mechanic told me that a big part of fixing cars is learning to listen. Car problems are too complicated and too idiosyncratic to diagnose from a checklist. An essential part of a mechanic's process is listening to the rhythms and sounds of an engine to diagnose the problems that are happening. Eventually the hood will open and the tools will come out, but before all of that happens, just *listen.*

In design, a playtest provides a situation to practice listening. Sit back and watch. When are the players leaning in and engaged? When are they leaning back and checking their phones? When are they exploding with laughter, and when are they silently focused? Which concepts are they grasping intuitively and which are sending them scurrying to the instructions? The more you practice, the better you will become at reading bodies, interactions, attention, emotion—the whole situation.

Through observation, it will become obvious that some aspects of your design are working smoothly and that other parts are far more unsuccessful than you had ever expected. At some point, your great ideas will inevitably run aground on the hard rocks of reality. It's a bracing experience to listen with honesty as your design falls apart. So bend to the process. Be flexible. Let the design evolve with the new understanding that listening gives you.

In opening up your process to the input of your playtesters, your sense of authorship expands to include other people. It's an ego-humbling experience to realize that fresh eyes can see things you can't and that you can fold their ideas into your own. The audience is your other. Learning to listen is a way of being, something you do over and over until it becomes part of your life. This is how design helps make us better people: as an ongoing practice that recognizes the humanity that surrounds us.

Just in case this sounds too much like preaching from the top of a mountain—full disclosure: I'm a horrible listener! Being attentive to others is most definitely not my forte. But I'm working on it.

PASSING IT ON

One of the very best ways to learn about design is by teaching others. Teach anywhere and anyone—it will make you a better designer.

This book is a cookbook of recipes for play and design. That may be true, but let's be honest: nobody ever exactly follows the instructions in a cookbook. A recipe is just a starting point. The best cooks improvise, making use of whatever is already in the kitchen, mixing and matching dishes and ingredients. This is exactly what I expect you to do with the exercises in this book: modding and redesigning them and making them your own. This process has a name. It is called teaching.

I sometimes get into arguments with friends who are worried about teaching. They feel like they haven't yet accumulated sufficient knowledge or expertise in order to instruct others. That's hogwash! In fact, they have the entire idea of teaching exactly backward. They shouldn't teach because they have arrived at some kind of endpoint. They should teach to learn about something, to get better at it, and to investigate it more deeply.

Teaching is how I have come to know what it means to design. It has given me a language for understanding and talking about what I do. Structuring a class, a workshop, or even a single exercise is an opportunity to figure out what design could mean. As you make something understandable to others, you yourself come to understand it more deeply.

The act of teaching makes you a better designer. On the job, you might be working on the same project for months or years. However, leading a single exercise, you may need to give meaningful feedback on a dozen different projects in the space of an hour. Sticking your head inside each one—trying to figure out what a designer was trying to do, what they actually did, and what you can say that's useful—it's exhausting! And exhilarating! It's training for your mind that makes you stronger and more flexible.

It's also important to note that teaching is full of incredibly enjoyable moments. The whole process—running exercises, facilitating collaborations, talking through difficult ideas—is creatively and intellectually stimulating like nothing else. It also offers the immediate gratification of helping fellow human beings. I'm not talking about being a professional educator—teaching can happen anywhere, at any time. You can play these exercises with your workmates in the office, with friends at a bar, or with kids at a birthday party.

How do you begin? Take a page from game designers like Jessica Hammer, Colleen Macklin, and John Sharp and start with the local context where you happen to be teaching. Ask someone to teach the group one of their favorite playground games. Play it together. Talk about it: What makes it fun? What could make it better? Then try out a modified version. Perhaps it breaks down completely, or perhaps you come up with something breathtakingly unexpected. Suddenly, before your very eyes, you are teaching.

Learning to teach encapsulates everything that is sandwiched between these covers. To listen to others. To expand your sense of self. To engage with the world. To come to know who you are. To bend to the process. To play, think, and design.

EXERCISES

WHEN YOU HAVE A DAY OR MORE TO DESIGN A GAME

FOUND OBJECTS GAME

A collection of strange and random objects are the creative prompts for quickly designing a game. A crash course in prototyping unusual forms of play.

O. Find some found objects

The one thing you need for the found-objects exercise is—you guessed it!—found objects. You can just gather the materials for this one exercise, but if you are running these exercises out of an ongoing program or space, it's worth your while to build a bank of objects that can also be used for a number of different projects. So think about building a collection of materials for prototyping.

Prototyping materials can include standard tabletop game supplies, such as:

- dice (regular 6-sided; more exotic ones too)
- cards (traditional decks of playing cards as well as blank playing cards)
- pawns and other game pieces
- tiles, tokens, wooden cubes, beads, and other little abstract pieces
- building blocks, small foam cubes, and other modular construction toys
- balls, beanbags, rope, cloth bags, small boxes
- sand timers, egg timers, Chess clocks
- sticky notes, index cards, writing utensils, scissors, tape, and other office supplies
- sketchbooks, markers, chalk, paper, and other art supplies

In addition, for this particular exercise you need to go beyond the list of conventional materials above and curate your own, more unexpected sets of objects. The best found objects lend themselves to a wide variety of uses. Each group of 3 or 4 designers will end up with 2 objects, so plan accordingly. Here's a short list of some of my favorites:

- a package of plain white T-shirts (pairs nicely with magic markers)
- an alarm clock
- a container of dried beans
- a trashy romance novel (or 3)
- a large and sturdy garbage bag
- a stack of plastic cups
- a roll of masking tape

Note that a stack of cups is a single found object, so each group should end up with 2 different items or sets of items. Remember, groups can always add more objects if they want a pad for scorekeeping or a die for a random roll.

What You Need

- Any number of players, working in small groups
- 1–2 hours (can be extended to a day or more)
- Traditional and untraditional prototyping supplies

What You Learn

- To rapidly prototype and playtest design ideas
- To explore the design affordances of physical objects
- Experimentation with unusual forms of interaction

DESIGN PROJECTS

FOUND OBJECTS GAME

1. Present the challenge

Divide everyone into groups of 3 or 4 people, and give each group 2 objects. You can pass out the objects yourself or have groups pick from the set. I like to have groups select objects for other groups—they can challenge each other with particularly strange combinations.

Then let them know what is happening. Tell them they have 15 minutes to create a game that they are going to share with the rest of the group. Their 2 objects have to play a central role in the game in some way. (Note: even though you are telling them they have only 15 minutes, you should actually give them 20 or 25. Time pressure will help them start prototyping before they otherwise might.)

They can make any kind of game they want, as long as it can be played in the context where you are running the exercise. It can be a game for 1 or 2 players, for a small group, or for everyone present to all play together. It's up to them.

2. Rapid design

Then they start designing. It might be a good idea to chat with them about some of the topics below before they start, but don't discuss too much in advance. Part of the value of this exercise is its ambiguity and open-endedness. The most important thing is that they are actively prototyping and designing as soon as they possibly can.

Discuss: What are affordances and how do you design with them?

What designers call affordances are the specific ways that an object lends itself to being used. A playing card, for example, can be shuffled into a deck, held in a hand with other cards, placed faceup or facedown, passed to another player, discarded out of the game, or even torn in half! Experimenting with the affordances of an object can help unlock possible uses and misuses and lead to interesting play. Remember, affordances can be social and cultural, not just physical: Are you more of a Queen of Hearts or an Ace of Spades? Encourage them to be inspired by playing around with their objects.

Discuss: What are some ways of going deeper than a game of pure skill?

As they start tossing objects around, there will be a strong tendency to create games of physical skill. It's only a matter of time until their design becomes throw-a-small-object-into-a-cup. Challenge them to go beyond simple carnival-style skill games. Can they build some kind of strategy into the game, so that what happened last round affects your decisions this round? Can they engender social relationships between players? For example, everyone works together against a powerful single player, or everyone is given a secret identity of some kind.

Discuss: How does a game's goal help shape and focus game play?

As they move from playing with objects to designing a game, it can be useful to talk about what differentiates a game from more informal kinds of play. For example, a traditional game has some kind of victory condition, an endpoint or goal or score to achieve. When one player (or a team or everyone cooperating together) reaches that goal, gets a certain score, or time runs out, then the game is over. Figuring out how a game ends can help evolve the looseness of just playing around into the more definite shape of a game.

Think about: Stop talking and start prototyping!

We all have a tendency to discuss possibilities and explore ideas through conversation. But because the time limit for this exercise is very short, they need to begin making and playing right away. Tell them to take the first half-decent idea that comes up and start trying it out. They should discuss things in detail only after they have had a chance to actually play something concrete.

As they design, walk around and check in with the groups. Make sure they are actively trying out ideas through play. Push and encourage them. Help them find the delicate balance between the productive intensity of a tight deadline and the devil-may-care freedom of free-flowing ideas. Emphasize that nobody is expecting them to make a polished, finished game design. What's more important is that they are actually doing something. It's completely fine if they end up with a partially finished game (perhaps it has some fun mechanics but not yet a victory condition).

About halfway through the design time, they should pivot from exploring lots of random ideas to refining and focusing their design into something they want to share with the rest of the group.

3. Play the games

It's important to not just share ideas but to play through every game that was designed, one by one. Depending on the number of groups, playing the games will take up about half of the total exercise time. Groups should *not* play their own games—they should teach it to volunteers from other groups to play. It's much easier to give feedback on someone else's design if you actually play it!

Discuss: What were some emotional moments from the others' games you just played?

Because this exercise emphasizes rapid prototyping, many of the designs will be half-formed ideas still emerging out of the larval stage. Focus on what is interesting about each prototype rather than on what is wrong with it. Did groups find unexpected ways to make use of their objects? What are the moments of enjoyment that start to happen when the game is played? Notice not just the game itself but also the behavior it generates: When were players exploding with emotion? When was the tension so intense you could cut it with a knife? Part of game design is crafting these moments of emotional experience.

Discuss: What were some of the more creative or unusual design ideas?

This exercise can be an interesting context for a discussion about creativity. There will undoubtedly be ideas here and there that break radically with the conventions of commercial game design. Perhaps players are put in an ambiguous competitive/collaborative relationship. Or maybe they have to move their bodies very slowly and carefully. Or just that everyone ended up laughing hysterically as part of the game. The exercise wasn't framed around being creative, but the weird objects, the time constraints, and the interaction with each other moved them into gloriously strange design spaces.

Discuss: How does it feel to officially be a game designer?

One of the most important lessons of this exercise is that anyone can make a game. Point out that in just 20 minutes, they managed to throw together some ideas that were not only playable and fun but also likely more interesting than most of what the industry churns out every year. It's empowering to realize that being a game designer is not just for overeducated experts or technical whizzes—anyone and everyone can be making games.

DESIGN PROJECTS

FOUND OBJECTS GAME

Variation: the start of something big

This one-hour exercise can easily be expanded into a multiday design project. The prototypes created in the first leg of the experience can then be taken home and iterated on further. I recommend not telling them at the start that their prototypes will be the basis of a longer project—it will keep them thinking in more experimental ways. For an added curve ball, add a third object after they share the initial prototype that will help them go deeper into exploring the possibilities of the design.

Context

A found objects game is a fantastic way to quickly jump into the process of iterating on a prototype. It makes a wonderful introductory icebreaker for a longer design class or workshop. The strange thinking forced by unusual objects takes even experienced designers out of their comfort zone—and challenges everyone to explore new ideas together.

Variation: one big group

A different version of this exercise can happen with everyone designing a single game together rather than splitting off into individual groups. To get started, stand in a big circle and put an unusual object (perhaps a rolling office chair) in the middle. Then start designing a game together through conversation. A first question might be: Who wants to demonstrate some ways of playing with this object? Talking through the process, you can explore affordances, add a goal, and iterate through prototyping. The advantage of this variation is that you can save a lot of time, since there is only one game to play at the end!

Variation: Iron Game Designer

Game designer Marc LeBlanc has used a similar strange-object constraint as the basis of something he calls Iron Game Designer, part of his legendary design workshops at the Game Developers Conference. The IndieCade Festival of Independent Games has run the same kind of event for years. Both are very similar to this exercise—rapid prototyping with unexpected objects and real-time pressure. A panel of judges evaluates the final games at the end, giving the affair the playful atmosphere of a game show contest.

MODDING A BROKEN GAME

Start with a simple 2-player card game; analyze the design, identify problems, and then fix what's broken. A guided tour through the entire design process.

MODDING A BROKEN GAME

What You Need

- Any number of players, working in pairs, in person or remotely online
- A few hours or a few days
- Decks of standard playing cards
- Game sheets, pages 152–153

What You Learn

- How modifying rules impacts the play of a game
- The challenge of communicating rules to a new player
- The iterative design process: analysis, prototyping, testing

0. Preparation

This exercise is based on 4 simple card games that use a standard deck of playing cards. Designers will be working in pairs, with a minimum of one deck for every 2 participants. However, it's a good idea to have more decks on hand in case some of the groups decide to expand the number of cards they put into their decks later on.

The game sheets contain the rules for the 4 games (War, Duo, Memory, and GOPS). Prepare paper or digital copies of the rules to give to each pair of designers, who will receive the rules for one of the games. Familiarize yourself with all of the games in advance—if possible, find a friend and play through them before running the exercise.

One quick note: this exercise works well as a quick design challenge that can be completed in a few hours, but it's also perfect for a longer project that can take place over a few days.

1. Play the broken games

To get started, divide everyone into pairs, and give each group a single page of rules and a deck of standard playing cards. (If you have an odd number, make a group of 3 and give that group rules for Memory, which works fine with 2 or 3 players). You want to have approximately equal numbers of groups assigned to each of the 4 games. It's fine if you don't end up using all 4 of the different games.

Let them play their game for about 10 minutes. The games take different amounts of time to play—the War groups won't finish a full game, and the others might be able to get through a few times if they play quickly. Even if they don't finish, in 10 minutes everyone should be familiar with their game's overall structure and flow. Be sure to answer and clarify any questions that come up about how any of them work.

2. Analyze the game designs

To begin the design process, each pair of designers will discuss and come to an agreement about what is wrong with their game. Depending on which game they were assigned, problems might include a slow and boring pace, a lack of meaningful or strategic choice, or randomness playing too large or too small of a role.

Each group should decide what they think are the 3 main problems with their existing design. Then spend a few minutes for some of the groups to informally share the results of their design analysis. It's not necessary for every group to discuss their analysis in detail, but having some groups talk about their thoughts and share their 3 main problems will help spark ideas for everyone.

Think about: Establishing a common understanding

In any group project, the most important thing is for everyone to agree, at least in a fundamental sense, about what they are trying to do. By finding common ground through a design analysis, the pairs establish a basis for the design work they are going to be doing together.

Think about: The subjectivity of design

This kind of design analysis—reflecting on one's own experience—is very subjective. Some might think that GOPS is about deeply rational strategic play, while others might feel that it is completely random. It may be particularly interesting to compare and contrast different analyses of the same game—do all of the Memory groups agree about what are the main design problems? It's OK if there are differences of opinion within a group, as long as there is general agreement about the primary problems.

Think about: Defining a design challenge

In agreeing on what is wrong with the existing design, each group is implicitly defining a positive goal— an aspirational target for a possible redesign. If a group thinks that there is no strategic choice in the game, then giving the game experience some meaningful strategy becomes one of their design goals.

Think about: Keeping things loose

This particular exercise is *not* about making a formal analysis with a set of defined problems and goals that the groups are permanently locked into. Things should feel fluid and improvised, and the groups should change and adjust their ideas about the game as they redesign it. If they discover new and unexpected things about the game as they continue to evolve it, that's a good sign!

3. Redesign, playtest, iterate

After the brief discussion, the heart of the exercise begins. Groups start changing some of the rules of their games and playing the new versions. To keep things constrained, I usually enforce these guidelines on how their designs can change:

- Each game needs to remain a 2-player card game.

- They can only use regular playing cards— they can't create custom cards. But they are welcome to add more standard cards and take cards out of the deck.

Within these constraints, there is a tremendous amount they can change. They can play with the turn structure, winning conditions, allowed player actions, the starting setup, the table layout, the number of each card in the deck, whether cards are faceup or facedown, etc. They can make a turn-based game into a rapid real-time game or even add narrative and role-playing elements.

Think about: How much change is too much change?

Is it possible to redesign the game to the point that it doesn't really resemble the original game that was being modified in the first place? The question will likely come up—but to be honest, it is a bit of a red herring. The main purpose of the exercise is for the designers to move through lots of iterations; they don't need to be too concerned with exactly how similar the redesigned games are to the starting version. Some of the final designs might end up being just subtle tweaks from the original and some might end up drastically different.

But to answer the question of how much change is too much, my rule of thumb is the *innocent onlooker test*. If someone outside the group of designers observed people playing the game, would they be able to point out which of the 4 original games it came from? If the game design has traveled so far away from its starting point that it would be impossible to identify the source, the design is no longer a modification but instead is an entirely new design. For the purposes of this exercise, that would be going too far.

A starting place for their redesign is to make a small change or two and see how it affects the gameplay. Does it begin to address

DESIGN PROJECTS

WAR

Setup

Shuffle the deck and deal each player half of the cards. Each player places their stack of cards facedown, in front of them.

You win War by having higher cards than your opponent and taking all of their cards.

Play

Each player turns over the top card from their stack at the same time. The player with the higher card takes both cards and puts them, facedown, on the bottom of her stack. A is considered the highest card, above K.

If the cards are the same rank, it is War. Each player then draws one card facedown and one card faceup. The player with the higher faceup cards takes both piles (6 cards). If the turned-up cards are again the same rank, each player places another card facedown and turns another card faceup. The player with the higher card takes all 10 cards, and so on.

Winning

The players keep playing, putting cards they win on the bottom of their stack. The game ends when one player has won all the cards.

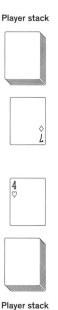

Player stack

Player stack

Setup

Shuffle the deck of cards and deal each player a hand of 7 cards. Put the rest of the cards in the center of the table as the draw pile. Turn over the top card and put it faceup next to the draw pile as the first card in the discard pile.

You win Duo by being the first player to get rid of all of the cards in your hand.

Play

The youngest player goes first and players alternate turns. On your turn, you play one card from your hand onto the discard. Your card must match the top card of the discard pile either in number or in suit. For example, if there is a 3◇ on the top of the discard, you can play any ◇ card or any 3 card (♣, ♠, or ♡).

You must play a card from your hand if you can. If you cannot play a card, you must draw a card from the draw pile into your hand. Once you play a card or draw a card, your turn is over.

Player's hand (kept hidden)

Draw pile   Discards

Player's hand (kept hidden)

Special cards

The face cards (J, Q, K) are special cards. Playing a special card still requires that you match with the top of the discard pile in color or number (except for K). Playing them has the following special effects:

J = Draw 2 cards
When you play a J, the other player must immediately draw 2 new cards from the draw pile into their hand

Q = Play again
After playing a Q, you can take another turn

K = Wild
You can play a K on any other card (Note that the next card must match the K in suit or be another K)

Winning

The first player to play the final card from their hand wins the game. If players go through the entire draw pile and both players have cards in their hands, the player with fewer cards in their hand wins.

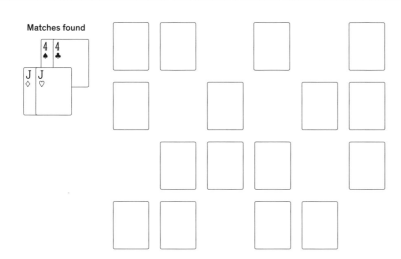

Matches found

Matches found

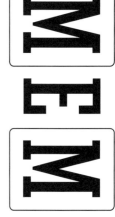

Setup

Shuffle the deck and deal the cards facedown in a random grid. You win Memory by finding more card matches than your opponent.

Play

Players alternate taking turns. The younger player plays first. On your turn, reveal 2 of the cards by turning them faceup. If your 2 cards are the same number and color (such as 7♡ and 7♢, or Q♠ and Q♣), then you have found a match. Keep the 2 matching cards and put them in your scoring pile. If they do not match, turn them back facedown.

Winning

When the players have taken all of the cards, the game is over. Count the cards in your scoring pile. The player with more cards is the winner.

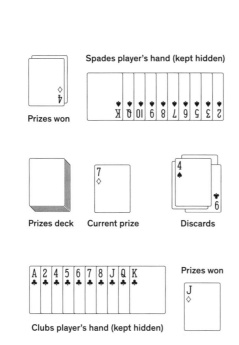

Spades player's hand (kept hidden)

Prizes won

Prizes deck Current prize Discards

Clubs player's hand (kept hidden)

Prizes won

Setup GOPS (Game of Pure Strategy) is for 2 players, using 3 suits from a standard 52-card deck. Cards rank from A (the lowest at 1 point), 2–10 (worth their face value), J 11, Q 12, and K 13 (highest).

The cards are sorted into suits: diamonds, hearts, spades, and clubs. Diamonds is shuffled and stacked facedown as a prize pile. Each player takes one of the black suits (spades and clubs). You can look at all 13 of your cards in your hand. Hearts are not used in the game at all.

You win GOPS by using your cards to bid on the prize pile cards that come up each turn.

Play The top card of the prize pile is turned faceup. Then each player selects any card from their hand with which to bid for it and places it facedown. When both players are ready, the bid cards are revealed simultaneously, and the higher bid wins the prize card. The bid cards are then discarded and the prize card is placed faceup beside the player who won it. The next card of the prize pile is turned faceup and players bid for it in the same way.

If the bids of the 2 players are equal, the bid cards are discarded but the prize card remains on offer. A new prize card is turned faceup and the next bid is for the 2 prize cards together, then for 3 prize cards if there is another tie, and so on. If the players' last bid cards are equal, the last prize card (and any others remaining from immediately preceding tied bids) is not won by either player.

Scoring When players run out of bid cards the game ends. Each player totals the value of the diamonds they have won in bids (A is worth 1 point, 2–10 face value, J 11, Q 12, and K 13), and the greater total wins the game.

the problems they identified? After a playtest, they can discuss what happened, propose new changes, and try them out.

Before too long, they will have slipped into an iterative design process, a cycle of making based on analyzing a design, implementing changes, and then playtesting those changes to see if they are headed in the right direction. When you iterate in this way, you explore the possible design space by way of bottom-up baby steps rather than through top-down master plans.

Since this is a short exercise, it may be enough that designers just play their own games as they are being developed. That said, playtesting each other's games and giving feedback can be incredibly helpful. Once they have some momentum with their prototypes, arrange a playtest. A natural grouping would be to have all of the designers working on the same original game play each other's designs (all of the Duo designers playtest the Duo variants of the other Duo teams).

Think about: Designing meaningful choices

The starting versions of the 4 games all share a fundamental problem: they don't give the player any real decisions. Each game manifests this challenge in a different way. In Duo, it is fairly obvious what the best move is each turn, so you never really make a meaningful choice. In War, the overwhelming randomness completely robs players of decision-making. The concept of meaningful choice is such a fundamental design concept that it's a good thing to talk about with designers as they work on their projects.

How do they make choices in their games more meaningful? Generally, by reducing "dead time" when no meaningful choices are happening while also expanding moments when players are engaged with engaging, tricky decisions. Perhaps they increase strategic options by making more information visible to one or both players (select your card from a hand or make both players' hands visible). Or they extend the outcome of a choice so that an action continues to have satisfying effects next turn (the suit that wins this turn can't be played next turn). Or perhaps the design can be improved on an experiential level by giving a game theatrical rituals that lean into the randomness (you don't just draw a card, you try to guess what it is).

4. Share final versions

Before the end of the exercise, each group writes up their final designs as a new set of rules. Because they have the complete rules for their source games, they already have a good template to use for the new versions. They should strive to make their rules logically complete, clearly written, and well-organized.

You definitely want to play through all of the games so that their designs can be experienced and appreciated. Don't have the designers play their own games—have them teach the game to others. Since all of the games use regular playing cards, if you want to get more people playing, it is not hard for multiple instances of the same game to happen at the same time.

Depending on the amount of time you have, consider some of the options below for structuring the final playthroughs and discussion:

- *Playing only by reading the rules.* If you have a small number of groups or a generous amount of time, you can enforce cold rules testing. That means the players can only look at the written rules and not get explanatory help from the designers. This will easily double the time it takes to try out the designs, but it offers wonderful (and wonderfully painful!) lessons in the challenge of effective communication.

- *Discussing clusters of games.* If you need to conserve time, one approach is to play through all of the games of a particular variation (such as all of the GOPS variants) back-to-back and then discuss them as a group. This can help highlight comparative approaches. What was common across multiple game designs? How diverse are the variations on the original game?

- *Simultaneous playtesting.* With large numbers of groups, there may not be time to discuss each individual design. In this case, multiple different games can be demonstrated simultaneously. For example, all of the groups that redesigned Memory can set up at different tables, and everyone else can circulate, trying out a few of the variations and observing others playing them. Then everyone can join in a comparative discussion of some of the variations before moving on to the next cluster.

Discuss: How did the modification change the experience?

Immediately after playing a mod, ask the playtesters to give their first impressions: What felt interesting or meaningful about the design? What changes to the rules resulted in unexpected outcomes in the play? Focus first on the interesting or positive aspects of the design, but talk about the shortcomings too.

Discuss: Did the mod solve the problems of the original game?

It's very likely that a design may have addressed some of the problems that were identified but not all of them. For example, a variation of War might have introduced player choice in an interesting way without yet managing to shorten the game to a reasonable length. Remind everyone that it's perfectly OK if the mod didn't fix everything—the whole point of the exercise is to practice solving design problems in a short period of time, not to arrive at a perfect conclusion.

Discuss: If work was going to continue, what are some possible changes?

The group can think about how the designers' intentions might be pushed even farther if the redesign work was to keep on going. What rough edges (confusing special rules or moments of less meaningful play) might be sanded down and polished? How could the design take the most interesting core ideas that are currently working and highlight them even more?

Discuss: What patterns emerged across the various game designs?

A part of the power of this exercise is that it reveals the breadth of possible ways to modify a particular core design. How many ways are there to make Memory better? The "theme and variations" component of the exercise reveals the essential mechanics of the source games, which were probably retained by most or all of the designs, and the wild new ways that a game can be reinterpreted through design.

Discuss: What did the designers find most challenging about the process?

After looking at all of the games, it's often beneficial to talk about the overall design experience. What parts of the process were unexpectedly demanding? Was it making creative decisions with a partner? The terror of playtesting an unfinished prototype? Or maybe figuring out how to communicate the rules? It's always interesting to see what different designers found challenging.

Variation: a remote situation

Instead of physical decks of playing cards, a website like playingcards.io can be integrated fairly easily into this exercise. The site gives you a virtual tabletop, where you can deal and shuffle cards, draw them into a hand, play them faceup or facedown, etc. You can even adjust the number of each card in the deck. The human players are responsible for the actual game rules as they manipulate the virtual cards, making it perfect for this kind of exercise.

Variation: solo design

Rather than working in groups of 2, each designer creates an individual game. The advantage is that every single participant must go through the entire process of testing, iterating, and writing out rules. There is nowhere to hide! To facilitate the process, each solo designer gets a playtesting partner to play and test each other's games in progress. Be warned: this approach doubles the number of designs at the end, so the final playtest and critique will take up a lot more time!

Variation: other kinds of games

You can run the structure of this exercise (play, analyze problems, redesign) with many kinds of games. This includes more complex board games, as well as simple folk games like Rock Paper Scissors, Tic-Tac-Toe, and 20 Questions.

Context

Modding a Broken Game is a classic design exercise: start with a game that needs improvement and then have designers try and make it better. The exercise works wonderfully as a first take-home assignment in a class or as a warm-up exercise at a workshop. Because the starting point is so well-defined, designers can quickly dig their teeth into trying out substantial design changes. Even veteran designers find this exercise quite challenging and can get a lot of benefit: it's always useful to practice fundamental design experimentation. And as a bonus, the final games are always fun to play.

DESIGN PROJECTS

DESIGN FROM CON- STRAINTS

A soup-to-nuts kit for inventing all kinds of design projects. The exercise walks you through ideation and iteration to presentation and critique.

0. Determine focus and constraints

To get started, think about what kinds of projects you want the designers to make. The constraints you select, more than anything else, will shape their experience. Below are some examples of constraints I have used in the past. Sometimes the group brainstorms them; other times I prepare them in advance. For examples of what prepared constraints can look like, the Designing from Constraints game sheets include constraint cards and explanations for the first project listed below. In all 3 of these examples, each group ends up with 2 or 3 different constraints (one each of the listed constraints) as a starting point for their design.

Example 1:
A project focused on mechanics and formal systems

First constraint: A material component. Each group gets to choose one materials card from a small deck. They list elements like dice, tokens, tiles, grid, etc. The material focus doesn't have to be the only component in the game— if your constraint is a grid, you probably want pieces or tokens to put on it—but it should be a primary part of the player experience.

Second constraint: A gameplay structure. A second deck of cards has different game mechanics, like a ticking clock, a one-versus-many structure, or real-time gameplay. Each mechanic includes a short description and example games that make use of the mechanic, with one primary reference game that the group is required to play.

Third constraint: A brainstormed theme. To guide the content of the design, the group brainstorms themes that they have never seen in a tabletop game before. I have seen everything from a political revolution to a robot sex clinic. A short phrase is all you need—brainstorm a list with the group, and write it on a whiteboard or otherwise in view of everyone.

What You Need

- Any number of players, working in small groups
- One or more weeks
- Prototyping materials
- Game sheets, pages 202–205 (as an example)

What You Learn

- The entire design experience, from concept to finish
- An iterative process via prototyping and playtesting
- How to create a design exercise for any situation

This is a butter, milk, and eggs exercise. Unlike a recipe limited to a single dish, Designing from Constraints gives you structures and processes that can be used to put together a whole banquet of different design projects. The particular examples mentioned here are for tabletop games and usually last for 2–4 weeks. You could easily adapt this exercise to other kinds of projects with different platforms, formats, and durations.

DESIGN PROJECTS

DESIGN FROM CONSTRAINTS

Example 2:
A project focused on social play
and experience design

First constraint: A social mechanic.
Play and discuss games that feature social
interaction and then brainstorm a list of
social play mechanics (bidding, hidden roles,
negotiation) that appears in the games you
discussed. For instance, coordination is a social
mechanic in Zen Counting, and coopetition is a
social mechanic in Wolves and Sheep.

Second constraint: Social emotions.
The group brainstorms a list of interpersonal
emotions that happen between people when
we play games with others, like jealously,
camaraderie, sympathy, deceit, etc.

Example 3:
A project focused on different ways
to tell interactive stories

First constraint: A short narrative.
Each group gets a different Grimm's fairy tale
or a Donald Barthelme short story. Another
approach is to give everyone the same text, like
Octavia Butler's "Bloodchild" (1995), and see all
the different ways there are to approach it. Note
that the design does not have to depict the entire
story; it can focus narrowly on a single moment,
character, or scene.

Second constraint: An interactive
narrative format.
Each group picks a format from a list
and receives a key reference game for their
format. Some examples are: interactive
book (Steve Jackson's Sorcery!); cooperative
simulation (Forbidden Island); game of social
intrigue (Love Letter); short role-playing
game (Lasers & Feelings); mystery puzzle
(Sherlock Holmes, Consulting Detective).

Think about: Carefully crafting constraints

These 3 examples are fairly general assignments
with quite open-ended projects. You could put together
much more focused guidelines, depending on your
needs. For example, constraints could be based
on a very particular format (an audio-only experience),
context (waiting room in a children's hospital),
or purpose (to help couples rediscover intimacy).

Think about: Any constraint will do

While constraints are important, don't fret too much
about crafting the perfect prompts. Perhaps the most
important function of constraints is to put arbitrary
limits on what designers can think about making.
Constraints help to narrow down the space of
possibility at the start of the process so that they are
not overwhelmed and paralyzed by too many options.
Constraints create a cognitive scaffold that helps
them be more decisive and quickly throw together
a prototype.

Rather than just handing out constraints, make a game of it. Groups can roll dice to determine who picks first. Or they can each be handed a random constraint but can trade with each other. Perhaps they "snake draft" 2 constraints from a list (pick the first constraint in regular order, and pick the second constraint in reverse order). If you let them choose, perhaps you tease them by only showing them a part of the constraint (like the first word of the short-story title they are choosing). Making a bit of ritual out of distributing the initial constraints establishes a nice sense of play at the opening of the project.

Think about: Providing an exercise brief

A useful technique is to pass out a summary of the entire project exercise—a page that lists the conceptual focus, the structure of the process, design tips, links to useful resources, etc. A formal brief ensures that all the information they need is in one place. Plus, writing it will help you think through the exercise in an organized way.

1. Present the exercise

To kick off the project, divide into groups and present the constraints. You might have designed the constraints in advance and just need to pass them out, or the group might generate a list of constraints through a brainstorm or discussion.

Think about: Group formation techniques

If they are going to work in groups, randomizing who works with whom is always a good way to go. The classic approach is counting off around a room (1, 2, 3, 4, 1, 2, 3, 4…), since it automatically breaks up cliques of people who are sitting near each other. If they are doing multiple projects over time, you might want to make sure different people end up together for each new project group. On the other hand, you can let groups form around common interests—for example, around one of the project constraints. Letting them choose their own groups can be more challenging, since social politics are always involved, and it's possible that some folks will be left out.

Think about: Having them brainstorm constraints

One advantage of having designers come up with their own constraints is that they will feel much more ownership over them. They can't blame you—they made the bed they are lying in! When brainstorming constraints, don't inform them in advance that they are generating their own limitations—it may put a damper on their creative weirdness. First have them generate a list of favorite birthday presents they ever received, and then tell them they have to pick one as the theme for their game.

2. Brainstorm, research, and prototype

These projects usually last about 2–3 weeks. That's not a lot of time! Rather than having a separate preliminary research phase, designers can be looking at references, reading articles, and getting inspiration at the same time that they also begin prototyping and iterating. Their goal is to put together a working prototype as soon as they can. My rule of thumb is that an interactive project should be playable within 20 percent of the total schedule, so if the project will last for 3 weeks, they should have an initial working prototype in about half a week.

DESIGN PROJECTS

DESIGN FROM CONSTRAINTS

3. Playtest and iterate

Every time you get together with the designers, they should have a new version of their project. The idea is to get into a rhythm—a cycle of playtesting, evaluation, and redesign. This iterative process is the beating heart of the exercise and where they spend the bulk of their time and effort.

Think about: Different kinds of playtesting

Whenever possible, they should playtest. The most important thing is for them to ask is: Why are they playtesting? What is the question that they hope their playtest will answer? As the project proceeds, playtesting usually evolves from informal prototype play to more formal and structured observational testing.

Think about: A guided brainstorm process

I often like to specify a technique that can help the group generate concepts that meet the constraints. The brainstorming exercises in the next section offer a variety of approaches. If they are working through several projects over time, you can mix and match techniques so that they get exposure to a variety of brainstorming methods.

Think about: A key research reference

When a group is trying to wrap their heads around a new design, it helps to have a common touchstone project to inform their thinking and discussions. If one of your constraints has to do with a design genre or format, consider providing each group (or letting them select) a key research reference that they are required to experience at the very beginning of the process.

Think about: Research throughout the process

In addition to a key research reference, think about providing readings, viewings, and other projects to provide fodder for discussion and inspiration. These kinds of research references are especially helpful for looking outside the confines of a particular field to see larger cultural implications of what they are designing. I love seeing game designers get inspired by culture that has nothing to do with games!

Think about: Integrating exercises

As the design process unfolds over a week or more, plan shorter exercises that have relevance to the project at hand. If it's a narrative project, perhaps they experience A Deck of Stories and Zombie Town. If the focus is on system mechanics, try Utopia 2099 and Trouble in Dodge City. Or if they are investigating social play, they might kick things off with Zen Counting and Wolves and Sheep.

Think about: A playtest log

One way for you to keep track of their process is for them to keep a record of their playtesting. Every time they playtest, they make an entry about what happened and the changes to the design that resulted. They can also record data (length of play, player feedback, ending game state) for each test in the log.

Think about: Finished versus unfinished materials

Set expectations for the final version at the start of the exercise—should they just make bare-bones "ugly" prototypes or more finished visual materials? Keeping things rough-and-ready allows them to focus on continual iteration of the core rules and system—but it's always useful to work on the visual and tactile experience too. If they work on several projects over many weeks, one approach is to have them start with more skeletal prototypes in the earlier projects and gradually emphasize more polished materials as they move on to later projects.

Think about: Gradually narrowing focus

The iteration process is an inverted pyramid. The very beginning is wide-open brainstorming and prototyping. Changes to the design gradually become more precise as the process morphs from experimentation to refinement. Pay attention to when this shift happens for designers. If they tighten up too early, they lose the opportunity to really explore the design space. On the other hand, if they start focusing too late, their final design may lack balance and polish.

4. Play and critique

When the exercise is finished, end with a final critique. When groups are making actual, playable projects, playing through each project should always be the basis of the discussion. The designers shouldn't play their own games—you and others should be playing them. Start playing first; let the conversation emerge during and after the experience.

Be sure to structure the critique time. Give each project the same amount of total minutes for playthrough and discussion. You might have to cut some of the longer projects short before you actually finish the game, but it's important that every project receives equal time for critique.

Also, thank everyone! Thank those who played, thank those who watched, thank everyone for comments and questions, and thank the designers for sharing their hard work and being open to critical feedback. Give the creators of the project a big round of applause. Then move on to the next project.

Think about: Defining the deliverables

Heading into the final critique, the designers should know what is expected of them. I like to include a complete list of the required final elements in the assignment brief. These might include a title and logline, a summary abstract, complete rules, a list of materials, photo documentation, and a brief written statement of their design intent.

Think about: Setting expectations

As the exercise winds down, there may be designers who are frustrated with their lack of progress. Often, they are comparing their work to commercially produced designs, which are designed over months or years, not a few short weeks! Remind them that in the time they were given, they can only really develop an early prototype. And in any case, a broken or unfinished experiment is almost always more instructive than something polished but boring. Celebrate weirdness and creativity, even when the design has not been fully resolved.

Think about: Product versus process

Despite this book's strong emphasis (perhaps overemphasis) on the design process, the final version of a project is important too. Not that everything must be perfect, but asking the design itself to be usable, coherent, and engaging is a way of practicing rigorous design. When they make things in the real world, they won't be around to explain why something is confusing or unfinished.

Think about: Cold playtesting

If you want to challenge their design communication, make the final critique a cold playtest. This means that the designers cannot explain what their project is and how it works; they can only rely on what they actually made, including any instructions and tutorial aids. This will certainly lengthen the critique as players struggle to learn the design, but if you can afford the extra time, it can be incredibly instructive.

Think about: Involving everyone

As much as possible, get everyone present to take part. This means asking for volunteers who are not the designers to play through the projects. (You should be playing too!) When the discussion starts, ask these playtesters to begin the conversation by sharing fresh observations from the playthrough that just took place. Rotate playtesting through the group so that everyone gets to play a game or two.

Think about: Managing the discussion

Establish a culture of thoughtful, supportive critique in which everyone sees feedback as a way of helping each other. During a critique, if the designers start defending their design against each critical comment, encourage them to speak less and listen more. They'll get much better feedback that way!

Think about: Outside critics

For a final critique, bringing in guests from outside the group can be helpful for getting new eyes on the projects and new voices in the room. Make sure they understand the context—the assignment, the process, the culture of supportive critique. After they play through a project, they can take the lead with critical feedback.

DESIGN PROJECTS

DESIGN FROM CONSTRAINTS

In terms of structuring a critique discussion, things will, of course, vary depending on the details of the exercise and the particular situation. Here are some good general go-to questions.

Discuss: What did the playtesters think?

The first people to speak up should be the ones who just experienced the design. Get their first impressions and design suggestions while they are still fresh.

Discuss: What were the highs and lows of the experience?

When did the playtesters cry out with emotion? When were they disengaged or frustrated? Are there any ways of doubling down on the good moments while also trimming away or minimizing the less successful elements of the experience?

Discuss: What aspects of the system felt difficult to learn?

It's always useful to think about which parts of a design are more intuitive to learn and which parts are more cognitively challenging for players to absorb. Even if the playtest was not a cold rules test and the designers verbally explained the instructions to the players, we can still talk about how to smooth the cognitive ergonomics. For example, if everyone kept on forgetting to draw a card at the end of their turn, would it be better if they drew it at the start of their turn instead?

Discuss: Are there any suggestions for improvement?

Based on what the designers were trying to accomplish, what might be changed to better reach their design goals? It's OK if there is disagreement here—different players might think the design should go in different directions. In any case, it's all speculation until it is actually implemented and playtested.

Discuss: What did the designers learn from the process?

The designers generally should listen to the discussion rather than jumping in to explain their design. However, before the critique is finished, ask them if there were any unexpected twists and turns in their creative process they want to share that might be helpful for others to hear about.

Variation: planning a whole course

Designing from Constraints is an exercise template that can be used to structure a larger workshop or class. String together a series of projects, each with a different conceptual focus, interwoven with relevant readings and shorter exercises—and voilà! You have a real design class. If they do several different projects, one way to end the class is to have them pick one of the earlier prototypes they worked on as a final project to polish and refine during the last section of the course.

Context

Designing from Constraints brings together many of the threads from other parts of this book: playing and brainstorming, iterating and playtesting, presenting and discussing. If you are planning a workshop or class, rather than working on a single project, it is usually best to work on several completely different designs over time. A series of short design projects helps everyone be less precious about perfection, moving rapidly through many ideas, each time facing strange new challenges and learning from past mistakes. Special thanks to Naomi Clark, Jesse Fuchs, and many other faculty at the NYU Game Center that have evolved the sample game sheet constraints over the years.

Designers make Passion Decks, each card naming something that interests them. They face off speed-date style, using the cards as prompts for a collaborative brainstorm.

PASSION DECK BRAIN -STORMING

PASSION DECK BRAINSTORMING

What You Need
- 2 or more players
- 45 minutes
- Index cards
- Blank paper (letter size and larger size)
- Writing utensils

What You Learn
- To develop new project ideas based on personal interests
- A collaborative model for creative idea brainstorming
- How creativity emerges out of constraints

0. Setup

You will need the following materials:

- 10 index cards for each participant
- Writing utensils—thick, colorful markers are highly recommended
- Letter-size or A4 paper, 2½ sheets per designer (10 designers = 25 sheets)
- Tabloid-size or A3 paper, 1 sheet per designer

A noisemaker or bell might come in handy to signal the end of a round. For the final part of the discussion, you will want a healthy section of wall space, along with painter's tape or pins. You can also just spread things out on tables.

1. Create passion decks

The main tool for this exercise is the Passion Deck, a small set of cards that represents things of interest for each participant. At the start of the exercise, hand out 10 index cards to each designer; on each card, the designer writes one thing that they are passionate about—whether professional or personal.

Think about: Keeping the decks unexpected

To help seed an interesting set of decks, I tell designers to make half of the cards inspired by things within the field and half from outside. So, for example, if everyone participating are game designers, half of the cards in someone's deck might contain more game-designery interests, like eSports spectatorship or one-button interfaces, and the other would be passions that are not directly about games, like spicy ramen curry or sustainable architecture.

Think about: Visual legibility

Keep the answers short! It's best if the cards have just a few words or a short phrase on them, not a full sentence. ("Spicy ramen curry" is only 3 words!) If possible, have them write in large letters with fat, juicy markers, not thin pens or pencils. The exercise is fast and furious, and each card should be quickly scannable.

2. Brainstorming in pairs

Arrange the group so that they are sitting in pairs facing each other. Each pair needs a letter-size sheet of blank paper in front of them, along with markers.

After each round, one of the designers rotates in a pattern, and everyone has a new partner, speed-date style. For example, if they are all sitting at a long table, perhaps one side of the table moves one seat to the left each time. Before starting, determine the overall rotation pattern and where everyone will move next. It's worth taking a few minutes to explain the rotation logic so that time isn't wasted figuring out where to go between brainstorming rounds.

Finally, everyone shuffles their Passion Decks and turns them facedown. By this point, they will all be chomping at the bit to start! Here's how to run the brainstorming:

Start! At the count of 1, 2, 3, GO! Everyone turns over their top card. Each pair should be looking at 2 cards—one from each of their decks. These 2 cards are the basis for brainstorming a project idea.

Discuss and record. They have 2 minutes to discuss, come up with a design idea based on the 2 cards, and write it on the sheet. On each sheet, all they need to write is a name for the concept, a visualization of some kind, and optionally some kind of short description. The visualization does not have to be polished! But drawing some kind of schematic or cartoon and not just writing words is important.

Stop, rotate, and repeat. After 2 minutes, ring your bell or turn off the lights or get everyone's attention in some other way. Immediately rotate to a new partner. On the count of 1, 2, 3, GO! the process begins again. Keep them moving quickly, and don't give them time to rest between brainstorms.

You can be collecting their previous sheets as they design. Have them ideate through 5 pairs (or more or less, as their energy and your needs dictate). Then move on to the next step.

Think about: The time limit

On the very first round, everyone will grumble about not having enough time. However, as they progress, they will get faster and faster. After a few rounds, if you see many groups ending early, reduce the time to a minute and a half, or even less! Just be aware of the overall group energy. It's important to keep up the time pressure as a constraint that helps focus their creative energy.

Think about: Keep things anonymous

You do not want to have the designers write their names on concepts they generate or otherwise own the sheets they produce. By not attaching themselves to a particular brainstormed concept, they will feel much more free to be weird and silly with their thinking.

DESIGN IDEATION

PASSION DECK BRAINSTORMING

3. Bigger-group brainstorming

After about 5 rounds of paired brainstorming, they move to groups of 3 or 4 designers. This may require a different seating arrangement and a different rotation logic. They will also use larger sheets of paper (tabloid or A3 size works well).

The brainstorming works as before, with the following differences:

- They have twice as much time (4 minutes instead of 2).

- Each designer presents a card, and so there will be 3 or 4 cards on the table.

- They don't have to use every card each time—but they should try!

- With the added people, space, and time, they can go into more detail—perhaps writing more notes inside the visualization to better explain the concept.

As much as possible, change up the composition of the groups. (It's OK if they end up repeating some partners.) Run these larger groups 4 times.

4. Pin up ideas and discuss

While they are brainstorming each time, you can be putting all of their sheets up on a wall. Or enlist everyone's help at the end to arrange them. With 5 rounds of pairs and 4 rounds of bigger groups, a group of 20 will generate a whopping 70 ideas, so be ready for the avalanche of concepts!

Once the sheets are pinned up or spread out on tables for view, give everyone a few moments to wander around and appreciate each other's ideas. After they have taken a look, discuss them as a whole. In general, ask people to comment on others' ideas that they see, not their own.

Discuss: Which ideas stand out as being unusual or intriguing?

Perhaps some are incredibly silly. Or complex. Or unexpected. What makes particular ideas interesting, even in this very raw and unrefined state?

Discuss: Which concepts catch your eye?

Some of the sheets of paper will pop out of the pack—why is that? Sometimes, it can come down to good handwriting or a clever idea expressed in a very simple way. Even though this exercise was not ostensibly about visual communication, seeing so many different concepts together becomes a wonderful opportunity to talk about how to make ideas quickly readable and visually enticing.

Discuss: What patterns emerge from the whole?

Looking at the collection of brainstormed ideas, are there any larger trends or other elements that appear across many of the ideas? Are there narrative themes or political issues that come up multiple times? What absence is surprising?

Discuss: What about the process was helpful in generating the ideas?

Because the brainstorm structure is itself a design, it's useful to think about what aspects of the process contributed to successful brainstorming. Was it the time pressure? Or the personal nature of the deck? The constantly changing partners? Or the consistent format of the sheet itself? Did the process get easier or more difficult over time? Always remember that everyone has a different creative process, and brainstorming techniques that work well for some designers might not work at all for others.

Variation: dedicated groups

If you already have groups that know they will be working with each other, you don't need to incorporate the speed-dating rotation component. A pair or small group might sit down together and go through several cards in their Passion Decks, generating a new concept each time that represents the interests of that dedicated group.

Variation: specialized decks

Rather than making decks based on personal interests, the content on the cards could be woven into a larger design or research process. For example, if you are solving a client's problem, one deck might contain a list of identified client needs. Or if you are generating story ideas, the decks might contain a combination of narrative references, unusual settings, and names of emotions that you want to be the focus of your story experience.

Variation: other people's passions

If your main aim is just to encourage strange and unexpected ideas, have designers swap decks with each other before they start brainstorming. Then they will really have to think on their feet. You lose some personal attachment to the cards, but you might get more deliciously bizarre results.

Context

This brainstorming technique can generate ideas for quick workshop prototypes or for yearlong thesis projects. Passion-deck brainstorming works as an icebreaker exercise for a group and can generate many unusual ideas in a very short period of time. It never fails to result in concepts that are highly creative but also represent the core interests of the group as a whole. And it never fails to leave a room full of delightfully inspired drawings and concepts.

5. Make use of the ideas

Presumably, you are using this exercise as part of a larger project generation process. What happens next depends on why they are brainstorming the concepts in the first place. Once the concepts are on the wall, you can use other mechanisms to determine group favorites. For example:

Voting. Each designer gets a handful of sticky notes or dot stickers to place on their favorite concepts. This is a quick way to determine crowd consensus about the most popular or promising ideas.

Spatial curation. Through a group discussion, rearrange and group similar concepts together. The groupings become a kind of mind map for the designers as a whole and could be used to define projects or ideas to pursue.

INVENT-YOUR-OWN B'STORM

Lots of ideas for generating ideas: a kit for inventing your own custom brainstorm process.

1. Design for the situation

This exercise is a general-purpose brainstorming kit that can help you craft the brainstorming process that fits your needs. In my experience, there are 3 general approaches to brainstorming, depending on who is involved and why you need to generate ideas:

Think alone, then share together.
Participants are given time to ruminate by themselves. After thinking on their own for a while, they then convene to share and compare what they came up with.

An oblique thinking process.
A structured series of steps that generates ideas indirectly to help think through a problem, like the creation of a collaborative group mind map.

On-the-spot invention.
The classic approach to brainstorming in which everyone rapidly thinks up ideas together, right there in the moment.

What You Need

- Any number of players
- Any amount of time
- Writing materials
- Index cards or sticky notes

What You Learn

- Techniques for putting together collaborative brainstorms
- Designing an ideation process based on needs and outcomes
- Being sensitive to different kinds of individual creative processes

DESIGN IDEATION

INVENT-YOUR-OWN BRAINSTORM

2. Establish constraints and execute

The devil is in the details. The examples below take the 3 general approaches and spin out each approach into 2 concrete brainstorm designs.

Think alone, then share together.
For designers who want time to think by themselves, this kind of approach gives them the space to do so. Depending on the situation, you might give them 15 minutes or a full week to think alone before they come back to share. Be warned: the danger of having everyone go off and think on their own is that some may arrive back at the share-together phase with complete ideas that they refuse to change or give up. The key is to structure the process so that they don't just reconvene and pitch finished ideas to each other. Be specific about what they think about on their own and how they share what they produced.

Think about: Different personalities

Every designer has a different kind of creative process. Some need peace and quiet and solitude in order to think deeply. Others can only properly chew on a problem while they are talking to teammates. Some respond well to orderly processes. Others are sparked by chaotic wildness. Be sensitive to these differences. One approach is to give participants a variety of methods over time so that they have a chance to explore and find the brainstorming process that works best for them.

Think about: Design the process

There is no right or wrong way to put together a brainstorming session. That said, a good brainstorm does not happen by itself. Carefully design what will happen, including constraints on input and output that will scaffold everyone's thinking. Without considerate design, brainstorm sessions can easily devolve into shouting matches where loud personalities dominate.

Think about: Design backward from outcomes

Start from where you want the brainstorm to end up. Is the point to generate lots of weird ideas? To dive deeply into understanding the problem? To develop group cohesion? The content generated by a brainstorm is not the only possible result—social and psychological outcomes are important too. Design the process that will get you there.

Think about: Don't overdesign

A brainstorm process should be loose enough to allow for playful misbehavior and unexpected accidents. Provide a structure, but encourage participants to deviate from the structure and make it their own. Feeling free and rebellious, silly and inappropriate are all important facets of creative brainstorming. Design it like you're putting together a party: make a plan, but don't try to guide it too much once it has its own momentum.

Example: Creative challenges
Rather than think of finished project ideas, when they think alone, each designer is tasked to come up with an abstract "creative challenge" that they want to tackle as part of the project. A creative challenge might be "tell a story without any characters" or "have members of the audience distrust each other" or "increase voter turnout in the city."

Creative challenges shouldn't be random—they should be generated in response to the particular design project at hand. They might take a structured form, such as one emotion, one interaction mechanic, and one impact on the audience's lives. When the designers reconvene, the creative challenges they brainstormed become the starting constraints for an on-the-spot idea brainstorm.

Example: Deconstructing project ideas
Go ahead and let the designers come up with full-blown project ideas when they think alone. When they reconvene, they take turns sharing their concepts, one project idea at a time. As one designer explains an idea, everyone else privately writes down one small thing they like about the idea on a card.

When everyone has shared their ideas, put all of the cards on the table. The collection represents elements of the various ideas that were interesting to someone else. Place similar cards together and look for patterns. Start to pull project ideas off the table by looking at combinations of card clusters. The approach of breaking apart existing ideas and remixing them together as a group helps everyone feel ownership of the concepts that emerge.

An oblique thinking process.
Rather than diving directly into idea generation, this approach gently steps everyone through a process meant to spark new and unusual kinds of thinking. The trick with an oblique thinking process is that the participants, at least temporarily, avoid directly solving the design problem. Instead, an oblique thinking process gives them a moment of cognitive pause during which they can stumble across new ideas that might not otherwise have occurred to them.

Example: Mind map
Start with a concept that is relevant to the brainstorming task at hand. For instance, if the project is about making a playful intervention into ordinary life, perhaps you start with a daily ritual—like brushing your teeth—that feels ripe for an intervention. Write the word or phrase on a large surface ("brushing your teeth") and draw a circle around it. Take turns writing down concepts that somehow relate to a concept that is already there, such as hygiene, a tingling sensation, or boredom. Draw circles around these concepts and connect them to the concept that gave rise to it. Each of these secondary concepts might then give rise to other words and phrases. Keep building the tree of language concepts until the writing surface is full.

Smaller groups can then "claim" a handful of circles by marking them with a color and brainstorming a project idea that uses the concepts in those circles. As the name implies, a mind map has the added advantage of extensively mapping out the conceptual terrain. It becomes a useful artifact for sparking new thinking throughout the lifetime of a project.

Example: World in an object
Prep this exercise by having everyone bring in a small personal object. After they spend a few moments examining their object, invite them write the following: 5 emotions or adjectives for the object; an imagined world where the object has a central role (a hero or a villain, a currency or a holy artifact); the central crisis or conflict in the world; and 3 ideas for story arcs set in the world.

Any tangible object is incredibly fertile ground for inspiration. There is its cultural meaning, the smell and texture of its materials, its manufacturing process, its functional use (or misuse)—so many different angles! This brainstorming exercise can work individually or in small groups, and they can swap the objects with each other too. Swapping objects provides the additional benefit of giving insight into the interests of others. Note that the example here is for a narrative world-building exercise, but you could also use objects with very different prompts for other kinds of brainstorms.

On-the-spot invention.
The traditional function of a brainstorm is to generate lots of possible project ideas. That's where on-the-spot invention comes in. Because constraints generate creativity, be thoughtful about how you design the brainstorm to focus and channel what everyone is thinking about at any given moment.

Example: Practical constraints
Come up with 4 vectors for defining possible project ideas. For a video game, this might be technical platform, target audience, core gameplay, and content theme. Distribute index cards in 4 colors and decide as a group which color will represent which category (blue = technical platform; red = target audience). Each participant privately brainstorms a few items for each category, writing them down on index cards of the appropriate color. Encourage them to go beyond traditional industry thinking for at least half of their cards Within small groups, separate the cards by color and shuffle each color stack.

Then turn over one card of each color and enjoy the strange random combinations of constraints. For example, smartphone + seniors who are dating + pet simulation + Dante's *Inferno*. Each group of designers comes up with one or more ideas together, based on the card constraints, and records it on a sheet of paper. Then deal another set of cards and generate another idea. Keep going.

Example: Just playing around
This approach works if the medium of the project is something that lends itself to open-ended, unstructured play, particularly physical play. For example, if you are designing a site-specific sport, show up at the site with a whole bunch of possible equipment (balls, hoops, ribbons, rope) and start playing around. If you are designing an experience for remote video conferences, get together in an actual online meeting and start goofing around with the platform's options and affordances.

As you proceed, someone in the group maintains a list of the interactions that the group came up with and what project ideas they suggest. The group cycles between periods of intuitive playing around and more focused conceptual discussion and idea generation, letting each mode of thinking inform the other. This approach takes time, as smaller experiential observations are gradually built up into more full-fledged concepts.

DESIGN IDEATION

INVENT-YOUR-OWN BRAINSTORM

3. Follow through

After you generate ideas, make the most of them. For example, if many groups are going through similar processes, it is always interesting to see what everyone came up with—sharing mind maps or card collections can help spark new ideas between groups. If the brainstorm is part of a bigger process, be sure to come up with actionable steps for moving things forward. After all, the idea is the easy part. The hard part is where you take it next.

Think about: There is no perfect idea

A misconception about brainstorming is that it will result in solutions to problems. It won't. A brainstorm, at its very best, produces starting points for a focused design process. Don't let the notion of finding the perfect idea or solution take hold. It will not only create expectations that can't be met, but it will keep everyone from sharing their silliest and weirdest ideas because they aren't measuring up to some imagined perfect standard.

Think about: Strategizing action items

When evaluating possible next steps after a brainstorm, one good selection criteria is to determine which concepts are most easily prototyped. The goal should be to move from the conceptual realm of brainstorming to the iterative realm of design as soon as possible. That can mean a group decides to prototype several different ideas as its next step, perhaps splitting up into smaller subgroups, each working on a different possible direction.

Context

Generating ideas well is its own special design problem, and requires as much design thinking as any other part of the process. This exercise is indebted to game designers Naomi Clark and Fawzi Mesmar, who have taught me so much about their own approaches to brainstorming and helped me organize my own thinking about it. This kit of brainstorming techniques is meant to be just a start—trust your instincts, experiment with different approaches, and see what works for you.

Think about: Clear instructions

Whatever approach you take, be extremely clear about the process. If you have a number of groups doing simultaneous brainstorming, detailed instructions will keep them focused and on track. This is particularly important if a part of the brainstorming process takes place on their own time, without anyone directly supervising.

Think about: Never owning an idea

One rule I like to impose when running brainstorms is that no one is ever allowed to refer to an idea by its author. There is no "Alina's idea" or "Diego's idea" —instead, it's "the procedural-interface idea" or "the quest-for-soba idea." As soon as an idea is spoken or shared, it enters the realm of the group mind. (And almost certainly, it was based on other ideas and inspirations that came from yet other sources.) By severing an association with a particular author, the idea will more easily achieve group buy-in, and whoever suggested it will be more open to changes and alterations.

You have 30 seconds to talk about an idea for a new project. Practice how to efficiently communicate a design and make it compelling for an audience.

ELEVATOR PITCHES

ELEVATOR PITCHES

0. Prepare for the pitch session

The idea of an "elevator pitch" comes from the storied scenario where you find yourself in an elevator with your boss. The clock is ticking as the elevator passes floors. Can you convey your groundbreaking idea before the elevator gets to her floor and she steps out?

This exercise is most useful during the early stages of concept development, when designers are still in the beginning stages of shaping their ideas. For example, after a project first kicks off, the designers bring an elevator pitch to the very next meeting.

Share the format of the exercise with them—they will each have 30 seconds to verbally pitch their idea to the group. No slides or visuals are allowed. It will be an informal presentation, but encourage them to prepare and rehearse in advance.

If you have the opportunity, a low-pressure practice elevator pitch can be a good way to break the ice. Have everyone go around the circle and pitch their ideal breakfast meal to the group. Or perhaps invent a summer blockbuster film and pretend to pitch it to studio executives. There's no need to give these warm-up pitches a detailed critique—the purpose is just to practice what it feels like to give a short oral presentation.

1. Present pitches and ask questions

One by one, each designer takes up to 30 seconds to share their idea with the larger group. There's no need to rush into a pitch—let each designer take a moment to breathe and begin whenever they are ready. Use a timer that will sound at 30 seconds after they begin speaking. It's not necessary to cut them off at that point, but it's useful to see which pitches ran long and which ran short.

Keep the session moving at a brisk pace. After each pitch, use the following questions for some rapid feedback and discussion and then quickly move on to the next pitch.

What You Need

- Any number of players
- A few minutes per participant

What You Learn

- How to quickly summarize a complex idea
- Practice in verbal communication
- Approaches for discussing project concepts

2. Discuss as you go

After a few pitches have happened, look for patterns and observations among several of them that highlight differences in how the designers are presenting ideas. I find that most designers go into a pitch session expecting to focus solely on the ideas. They often find it a refreshing surprise to talk at least as much about how they presented as what they presented. Of course, it goes without saying that the pitches should also get feedback on the actual design ideas!

Use the following questions as feedback on individual pitches or save them for a final discussion during which you can compare and contrast different approaches.

Discuss: What questions immediately come to mind?

As soon as a pitch finishes, I like to ask the group what questions are lingering in their heads about the pitch they just heard. In other words, what was ambiguous or confusing about the pitch? For example, if the concept pitches a game but it's unclear whether it's played on a smartphone, a television, or a tabletop, it is difficult to get a clear picture of the idea.

Discuss: On a basic, factual level, did the pitch manage to express the concept?

This is the *WHAT* of the pitch. Was the general outline of the idea clearly conveyed to the listeners? Making sure the basic facts of an idea were communicated addresses perhaps the most important aspect of a pitch: conveying information.

Discuss: Beyond the facts, is it clear what is innovative, important, or distinctive?

Beyond the *WHAT*, this is the *WHY* of the pitch. Game designer Colleen Macklin always asks her students: What is cool about your idea? Ask yourself: Does the pitch have the Colleen Macklin Factor—are you sufficiently conveying the coolness of your idea? The why of a pitch might be personal, political, technical, financial, narrative—as long as it is in there.

It is extremely hard to successfully squeeze everything into a 30-second pitch! It is common, for example, that a presentation lists facts and features (the what) but doesn't manage to explain the compelling reason for the project to exist (the why). That very intense challenge is, in fact, exactly what this exercise practices.

Discuss: What are some of the ways you can start a pitch?

How can an audience be led into the idea? Does the pitch present a problem and solution? Or does it start by spinning a tale about a fantastical world? Or tell an anecdote about a personal struggle? The beginning of a presentation should immediately hook the listener and entice them to want to hear more.

Discuss: Did any of the pitches successfully use humor?

Putting a smile on the faces of the audience is a great way to engage with them. The tail wags the dog: if we're smiling, we're going to enjoy what we hear. Cheesy and gratuitous humor can definitely fall flat, but if there is a way to get everyone chuckling, it can be a strong opener.

Discuss: Were there any interactive moments during the pitches?

Asking a question—even a rhetorical one—is a fantastic way to gather up the attention of people sitting around a table or at an online meeting. Perhaps you take a quick poll, or ask everyone to imagine something from their childhood, or ask them what they would do in the protagonist's situation. Perhaps you can even (somehow!) demo a brief moment of play.

DESIGN IDEATION

ELEVATOR PITCHES

Context

Learning how to quickly present a concept is a key skill for any kind of designer. This exercise is about practicing clear articulation of a design while also leveraging the act of communication to assist in the creative process itself. The core lessons of the exercise—for example, making sure that both the *what* and the *why* are being conveyed—are valuable not just for short pitches but for any kind of verbal or written communication.

Discuss: Did the pitches manage to paint a clear picture?

An almost-universal goal of a pitch is to paint a clear picture in the heads of the audience. Use experiential, visually descriptive language to conjure a vivid image of the project. Painting a clear picture ensures that everyone hearing the pitch is on the same page about what the project looks and feels like. It will be much more memorable too!

Discuss: Did any of the pitches make good use of ambiguity?

A common mistake is to nervously cram too much information into a presentation. During a 30-second pitch, there's no need to give complete details on everything. You are conveying the basic core idea along with a bit of what makes it special. It's OK to leave things out, to intrigue the listener into wanting to know more.

Discuss: Which pitches were able to describe a moment of experience in detail?

When pressed for time, we tend to talk in generalized abstractions. Yet the very opposite—getting into concrete details—is so much more effective in conveying ideas. If you can convey one specific moment that encapsulates the core experience—perhaps a key instance of user choice—it can be incredibly effective.

Discuss: Which pitches—and which designers—were most memorable?

There is no one correct way to pitch an idea. Some designers enjoy the hard sell. Others are more like stand-up comics. Still others emphasize the high-concept artistic intention. The personality of the pitch depends on the project, your audience, and your own persona as a designer. It's something you can only figure out through practice.

Brainstorm the qualities of what makes a good teammate. The resulting list challenges everyone involved to become a better collaborator.

A GOOD COLLABO -RATOR

A GOOD COLLABORATOR

1. Brainstorm a list

This exercise is for any situation in which designers will work in groups on a project for more than a single session—perhaps a few days, a few weeks, or more. To begin, gather everyone to brainstorm the qualities of a good collaborator. If they have trouble coming up with ideas, ask them to think about the positive qualities of people with whom they have collaborated in the past: What made them good teammates?

As they shout out answers, take notes somewhere visible to everyone, whether on a whiteboard or on a digital document that everyone can see. Once you have a substantial set of responses, combine similar ideas to generate a streamlined list of the qualities of a good collaborator.

Here are a couple of lists that second-year undergraduate students at the NYU Game Center generated—if only all of our collaborators could have every one of these amazing qualities!

- A good listener

- Someone who actively communicates and is responsive

- Open-minded to others' ideas / don't insist on your own ideas—take a step back

- Diplomatic if something goes wrong (not accusatory—no blaming, no shaming)

- A hard worker—don't leave everything to your partner but also keep partners accountable

- Respectful of work that has been done / be honest with feedback

- Respectful of personal boundaries— understand time and workflow and don't overload yourself or partners with too much work

- Communicate/understand everyone's strengths and weaknesses, both for breaking up work tasks and for being confident within the group

What You Need

- One or more groups working on projects
- 15 minutes
- A physical or digital writing surface

What You Learn

- A way for a group to agree on a collaboration process
- What everyone values in working with each other
- How to create a constitution that can hold a creative group together

- Be a good communicator—make a place to track progress, check to make sure that everyone is on the same page, make sure everyone is heard

- Be open to compromise—be flexible, don't hold on to ideas too much, be open to change, don't be precious about not changing ideas

- Say yes more—be positive, flexible, don't just shoot down ideas

- Be responsible—be on time for meetings, finish when you said you would, have good time management skills, understand how long a task will take

- Be sensitive to different situations and expectations

- Be realistic with goals—can you meet your tasks and deadlines?

- Be engaged (but not overengaged) with the project

. Use the list

Once the list has been generated, let everyone know that they have just created the standard for which they will now hold themselves accountable. These qualities are what each of them will strive to embody as they work together. Moving forward, make sure that everyone has a copy of the list. You can keep it in a shared digital document or even print it out as a poster for the workspace.

Periodically, remind them to review the list as a way of holding themselves accountable. This might happen, for example, after a group has been working together for a few weeks. Within a group, allow everyone to share the ways that they can improve and be better collaborators. They are not permitted at that moment to talk about their collaborators (to avoid defensive confrontations). They can only talk about how they themselves can get better: self-improvement is the focus, not finger-pointing.

Think about: Conflict resolution

If there is tension or conflict in a group, leverage the list as the common ideal for which everyone strives. Have groups frame critical comments in terms of the list: point out which list items represent areas for improvement. Remember to structure these conversations with a self-critical rather than an accusatory approach—it is much easier to address problems if people can admit to them without being prompted.

Think about: Updating the list

Periodically remind everyone about the list, read through it, and ask if anyone has suggestions for additions. It's very possible that new collaboration experiences will lead to new items for list.

Think about: A group constitution

Rather than a single list for all of the groups, each small group can create its own list of what makes a good collaborator. This variation is especially helpful for extended projects on which people will be working together over long periods of time. The group list of traits can be combined with a project mission statement or set of agreed-upon creative challenges. The resulting document is a kind of group charter that defines how the designers want to work together.

Context

This incredibly simple exercise is surprisingly effective. Too often, discussions about proper collaboration focus on negative qualities to be avoided rather than positive, aspirational attitudes and behaviors. The list can create a wonderful sense of shared community: holding everyone accountable to a standard becomes easier when everyone takes part in defining that standard. This exercise is inspired by *The Assertiveness Workbook*, by Randy J. Paterson, and by the emotionally nuanced teaching approaches of artist/designers Matt Boch and Marie Claire LeBlanc Flanagan.

DESIGN COLLABORATION

KEYWORD VISION STATEM'T

Everyone brainstorms keywords, which then are put into a common mission statement. A collaborative writing exercise to build group cohesion and a shared project vision.

1. Individually generate keywords

This exercise is about establishing a group vision early in the design process. It is best applied at the beginning, when the general outlines of a project are known but the detailed work has not yet begun. (For example, ideas have been pitched and groups have just been formed around them.) It can help everyone understand why people were attracted to the idea, what they are working on, and how to move forward together.

To get started, each group member thinks about what excites them most about the project and privately writes down a word or a 2–3 word phrase on an index card. For smaller groups (5 or fewer designers), everyone can write 3 or 4 cards. For larger groups, writing 2 cards is fine. Limiting the number of cards forces people to really think about what interests them the most.

Think about: A range of motivations

While people think about what to write on their cards, remind them that there is no right or wrong answer. There might be technical or formal challenges that interest them, narrative or experiential components of the project, or cultural and political topics. For a game I was helping to design based on the infinite library of Jorge Luis Borges, group members came up with cards that ranged from "language-based gameplay" and "metaphysical fable" to "spooky mood" and "procedural level generation."

What You Need

- Any number of groups working on a project
- 20 minutes
- Index cards
- Markers
- Large paper sheets or whiteboards

What You Learn

- How to collaboratively craft a group mission statement
- Communicating design ideas through writing and language
- Fostering shared group ownership of a project

2. Share and combine

Everyone shares their cards by placing them faceup on a table and talking through what they meant by each card. Likely there will be a lot of overlaps!

The next step is to combine as many of the cards as possible into a 2–3 sentence vision statement. The collective statement must include at least one card from each group member (or at least 2 per member for smaller groups).

The statement must use the exact text from the cards. Other words can be added to link the card text together, and it's OK to change tense for grammatical agreement. The statement can take the form of: "[Project title] is..." For example, "The Infinite Library is a game that uses

DESIGN COLLABORATION

KEYWORD VISION STATEMENT

Think about: Oblique keyword prompts

A project might not have enough of a focused identity for designers to think up an initial set of keywords. In that case, try using a more oblique prompt for the keywords. For example, working with a group of professors who were designing a new degree program around video games, I had everyone think about positive emotional experiences they had with games in their lives (including sports, tabletop games, crosswords, etc.). Those emotional words became the keywords for a vision statement about the curriculum. The results were much more interesting than if they had generated keywords more conventionally.

language-based gameplay and procedural-level generation to tell a metaphysical fable with a spooky mood."

Combining the language into a few sentences that flow well together is actually a very challenging puzzle. That bit of linguistic intrigue helps distract everyone from the fact that they are forging a group statement that reflects everyone's contributions. If some cards are very similar, there's no need to use them all.

The final statements should be written up on a whiteboard or large sheet of paper, or perhaps put into a shared digital document. Take a look at everyone's and compare. Which vision statements feel the most compelling or exciting or unexpected? Do the groups feel that the statements capture what they want to design? What were the points of agreement and disagreement among everyone's cards? Did the process of composing the statement open up any new ideas or possibilities?

Think about: Cross-group editing

As an additional step, focus on crafting the language of a vision statement. Write each statement on a whiteboard or editable document and let members from different groups edit each other's draft statements. The edited version does not need to stick to the words on the original keyword cards, which means that the editing can really focus on clarity and flow.

Think about: For very large groups

If you have a lot of people working on a single big project, divide into smaller groups, with each group making their own vision statement for the project. Then share them, together. This can be an eye-opening way of realizing the diversity of ideas in the room and the wide range of ways that a vision statement for a single project can be expressed.

3. Keep the statement handy

As a project evolves and changes, there are always questions about the direction it should go. A vision statement can act as a conceptual anchor to ground the overall creative mission of the design. When considering new features, consult the vision statement: Does the possible new direction move the core vision forward? Or is it a distraction that will cost production time without really getting to the heart of what the project is about? Of course, the vision statement for a project can always change and evolve too!

In a larger organization, keeping everyone aware of project vision is key. Fawzi Mesmar, who runs design departments for some of the largest video game developers in the industry, has "design pillars" printed on posters and spread throughout the office so that his team (and everyone else!) is constantly reminded about the project intent.

Context

Boiling down the core of a complex project to a simple statement is an incredibly important exercise—it creates group cohesion, helps resolve future decisions, and can communicate the project to the outside world. I have used this exercise with teammates on commercial projects, with design students working on new games, and with staff at nonprofits refining their organizational goals and mission. It works.

GAME SHEETS

	1	2	3	4	5	6
1						
2						
3						
4						
5						
6						

DIE
vs.
DIE

2   4   6

1   3   5

GET OUT!

	0	1	2	3	4	5	6	7	8	9
0										
1										
2										
3										
4										
5										
6										
7										
8										
9										

#	Notes

GET OUT!

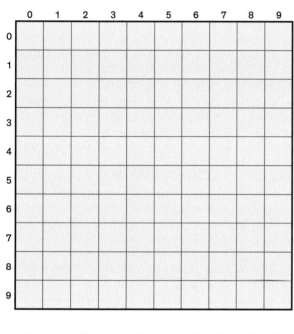

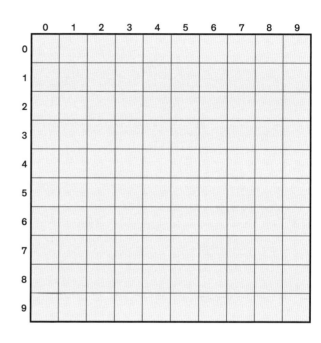

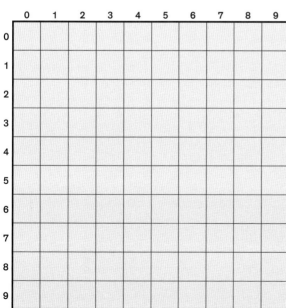

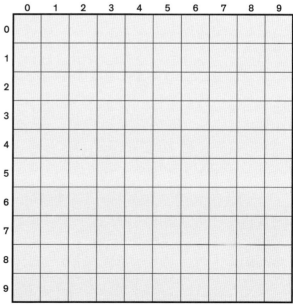

GET OUT!

—— GAME ELEMENTS ——

 Ute

She moves in a straight line and stops when she hits something

 Exit

Move Ute to this square to GET OUT and beat the level

 Wall

This stops Ute from moving

 1

2

3

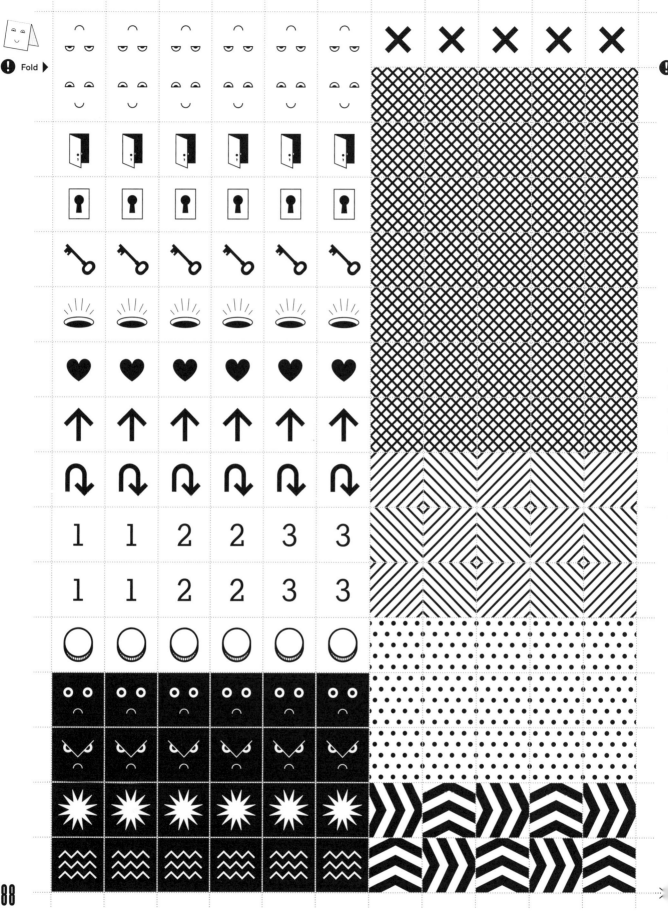

GET OUT!

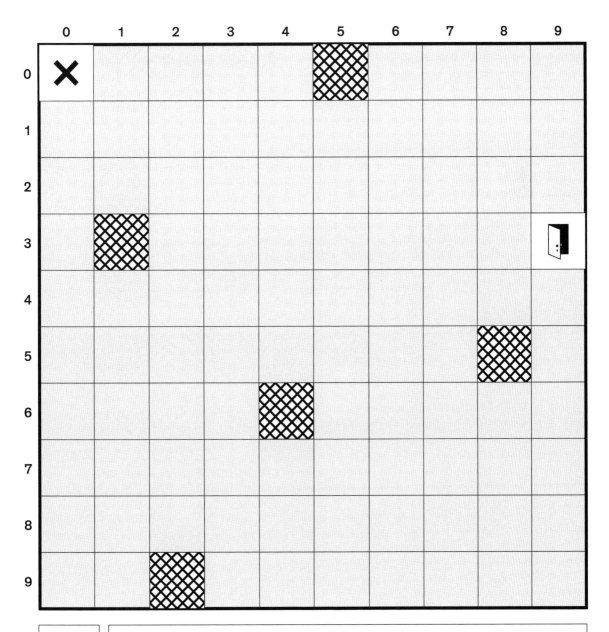

#	Notes

To Play

Each player rolls 2 dice.

Resolve lower numbers first, according to the dice chart.

Winning: at the end of a turn, if a player has 10+ happiness, the player with the most happiness wins the game (if it's a tie, play another turn).

- ⚀ **FARM** +①happiness
- ⚁ **ARTIFACT** +②happiness
- ⚂ **WALL** Defend ① Raid for this turn
- ⚃ **WALL** Defend ① Raid for this turn
- ⚄ **RAID** Opponent without wall loses ① happiness
- ⚅ **THIEF** Steal ③ happiness from opponent

To Balance

Change any circled number.

Change which die numbers do which actions.

You can eliminate actions (i.e., no FARMS) but THIEF must stay only at 6.

No changes to core logic or rules for winning.

Utopia 2099

⚀	
⚁	
⚂	
⚃	
⚄	
⚅ **THIEF**	Steal ◯ happiness from opponent

Utopia 2099
Experts

To Play

Each player picks a different expert.

For numbers 1–5, use your balanced version.

A 6 means your expert power happens (two 6s means it happens twice).

To Balance

The power of the THIEF remains the same.

Modify any of the expert powers.

You can completely redesign one expert (except for the THIEF).

Criteria

Power balance (equal chances of winning).

Each one is enjoyable and exciting to play.

The ability feels right for the narrative identity.

THIEF	Steal ◯ happiness from opponent
HISTORIAN	Reroll both dice and take both actions
ENGINEER	Raid with a strength of 2 (opponent loses 2 happiness)
SPY	Next turn, opponent does not roll at all

TROUBLE IN DODGE CITY

Setup

Count 10 tokens for each player and put them in a single central loot pile.

Shuffle the cards into a facedown deck.

Deal a hand of 3 to each player; keep your hand hidden.

Play

Oldest player goes first; take turns clockwise around the table.

On your turn, draw a card and play a card; see chart below.

Then discard the card you played unless another rule tells you to keep it.

Play:	Action:
1 OUTLAW	Take 1 token from any other player.
2 SALOON	Keep the saloon out in front of you: for each saloon already out at the start of your turn, draw +1 card and play +1 card.
3 MERCHANT	Take 3 tokens from the central loot pile.
4 SHERIFF	Take 4 tokens from the central loot pile.
5 MAYOR	Take 5 tokens from the central loot pile.

End

The game is over immediately when there are no more loot tokens in the central pile.

The player with the most loot tokens wins.

TROUBLE IN DODGE CITY

Setup

Count 10 tokens for each player and put them in a single central loot pile.

Shuffle the cards into a facedown deck.

Deal a hand of 3 to each player; keep your hand hidden.

Play

Oldest player goes first; take turns clockwise around the table.

On your turn, draw a card and play a card; see chart below.

Then discard the card you played unless another rule tells you to keep it.

Play:	Action:
1 OUTLAW	Take 1 token from any other player.
2 SALOON	Keep the saloon 2 out in front of you: for each saloon already out at the start of your turn, draw +1 card and play +1 card.
3 MERCHANT	Take 3 tokens from the central loot pile.
4 SHERIFF	Take 4 tokens from the central loot pile.
5 MAYOR	Take 5 tokens from the central loot pile.

End

The game is over immediately when there are no more loot tokens in the central pile.

The player with the most loot tokens wins.

1	1	1	1	1
OUTLAW	OUTLAW	OUTLAW	OUTLAW	OUTLAW
2	2	2	2	2
SALOON	SALOON	SALOON	SALOON	SALOON
3	3	3	3	3
MERCHANT	MERCHANT	MERCHANT	MERCHANT	MERCHANT
4	4	4	4	4
SHERIFF	SHERIFF	SHERIFF	SHERIFF	SHERIFF
5	5	5	5	5
MAYOR	MAYOR	MAYOR	MAYOR	MAYOR

2× Make 2 copies of this page for 1 full deck

BOLF!

Your name: _____

Hole	Score (A+B)	Most Fun	Most Creative
1	_____	☐	☐
2	_____	☐	☐
3	_____	☐	☐
4	_____	☐	☐
5	_____	☐	☐
6	_____	☐	☐
7	_____	☐	☐
8	_____	☐	☐
9	_____	☐	☐
10	_____	☐	☐
11	_____	☐	☐
12	_____	☐	☐
13	_____	☐	☐
14	_____	☐	☐
15	_____	☐	☐
16	_____	☐	☐
Avg.	_____		

Basic Rules

Stand on starting X and toss beanbag.

Stand where it landed and toss again.

Finish hole when beanbag touches ground inside hole.

Score is number of tosses.

Design a Hole

Make it a unique experience (you can add stroke penalties and special rules).

Design 2 holes:
- an easier tutorial hole "A"
- an advanced hole "B"

The stroke par for both holes must add to 7.

Create clear, self-explanatory instruction signs. (You will not be around when your hole is played!)

Tournament

Play as many holes as possible.

Fill out a scorecard for each hole you play by adding up your total score for A+B.

Max score for a hole is 14 (double par).

Vote for the most fun and most creative holes that you played.

Winning

Individual:
- the lowest average score

Teams:
- the hole with closest average to par 7, plus awards for most fun and creative

BOLF!

Your name: _____

Hole	Score (A+B)	Most Fun	Most Creative
1	_____	☐	☐
2	_____	☐	☐
3	_____	☐	☐
4	_____	☐	☐
5	_____	☐	☐
6	_____	☐	☐
7	_____	☐	☐
8	_____	☐	☐
9	_____	☐	☐
10	_____	☐	☐
11	_____	☐	☐
12	_____	☐	☐
13	_____	☐	☐
14	_____	☐	☐
15	_____	☐	☐
16	_____	☐	☐
Avg.	_____		

Basic Rules

Stand on starting X and toss beanbag.

Stand where it landed and toss again.

Finish hole when beanbag touches ground inside hole.

Score is number of tosses.

Design a Hole

Make it a unique experience (you can add stroke penalties and special rules).

Design 2 holes:
- an easier tutorial hole "A"
- an advanced hole "B"

The stroke par for both holes must add to 7.

Create clear, self-explanatory instruction signs. (You will not be around when your hole is played!)

Tournament

Play as many holes as possible.

Fill out a scorecard for each hole you play by adding up your total score for A+B.

Max score for a hole is 14 (double par).

Vote for the most fun and most creative holes that you played.

Winning

Individual:
- the lowest average score

Teams:
- the hole with closest average to par 7, plus awards for most fun and creative

VOLF!

The Turnaround

Tutorial Hole

SETUP
- Place your cup.
- Take 1 step away from the cup and put the ball on the floor between your legs.

SPECIAL RULES
- You must face away from the cup and flick the ball between your legs.
- If you miss, return the ball to the setup position.

Advanced Hole

SETUP
- Place your cup.
- Take 3 steps away from the cup and put the ball on the floor between your legs.

SPECIAL RULES
- Same as the tutorial hole

Looper

Tutorial Hole

SETUP
- Place your cup and start with the ball touching the "front" of the cup.

SPECIAL RULES
- The ball must touch the "back" side (the opposite side of the cup from the starting location) to score.

starting "front" side   scoring "back" side

Advanced Hole

SETUP
- Place two cups at a distance of 2 steps from each other.
- Place the ball on the "front" side of one cup facing the second cup.

SPECIAL RULES
- The ball must travel around the second cup and touch the "back" of the first cup to score.

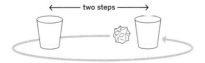

two steps

Materials

- One letter-size piece of paper, wadded into a ball
- A drinking cup (about 3½-inch diameter)

Basic Rules

Your goal: flick the paper ball to touch the side of the cup in as few moves as possible.

Set up the cup and yourself according to the rules of the hole.

Flick the paper ball with your index finger toward the cup—your next flick takes place from that new location.

Count your flicks—when the ball hits the cup, that is your score (it does NOT have to go in the cup—just touch the side).

Hole instructions can add special rules.

Design a Hole

Make it a unique experience.

Define where the cup starts relative to the player.

You can include simple objects and elements that are likely to be in the spaces of other players (a chair, a second cup, a pencil, etc.).

You can add special rules and golf-style penalties involving the space, the way that the player has to flick the ball, etc.

Design 2 holes using the same gameplay mechanic
- an easier Tutorial hole that teaches the mechanic
- an Advanced hole that adds more challenge

The number of flicks for both holes should add to par 7 on average.

Create instructions for your hole and put them in the group folder—these will be the ONLY explanation, so make them clear!

Tournament

We will create a spreadsheet for everyone's holes—add your hole to the spreadsheet.

Start playing other designers' holes (if you don't have the space or equipment, that's OK—just try a different hole).

When you finish a hole, put your flick count into the spreadsheet for the tutorial and the advanced hole.

After we are all finished, vote for the most fun and most creative hole (you can't vote for your own).

Final Tally

The winning player is the one with the lowest average score.

The winning designers are the ones whose hole has an average score closest to 7, plus the holes with most votes get the awards for most fun and most creative.

Deck of Stories

Cut this out and fold
into quarters to make
a mini book cover.
The first and last pages
are folded inside:

The title is folded outside:

Cut out the story deck
from the following pages.

The End

Adam, Eve, and the serpent
lived in the garden.

Life in
the
Garden

God was not pleased.

And Eve laughed
to herself.

All the creatures
in the garden
went to sleep.

Then the sky grew dark.

So at last the serpent
was happy.

Adam refused to speak.

And the trees
in the orchard
bore fruit.

Many days passed.
Too many to count.

And Eve
dug a hole in the earth
of the garden.

She climbed inside
and slept
for a very long time.

And with a branch
that had fallen
from one of the trees
in the orchard
Eve hit the serpent
on the head
many times
and with great strength.

But we all know
how difficult it is
to kill a serpent.

And high above
the moon
and the sun
chased each other
around the earth
like giddy lovers.

Then the garden
grew quiet.

God remained silent.

And so the story thickens.

And the serpent
drew a map
of the garden
by tracing lines
in the earth
with the thin stylus
of his body.

And so
the serpent realized
with a shudder
that the garden
was not a garden.

Once Adam found
a piece of fruit
that had fallen
on the ground.

He picked it up
threw it into the sky
and to his astonishment
it never returned
to the earth.

But that is only
what the serpent
has told me.

And who really
can believe
the slim words
of a serpent?

One day Adam cried.
Eve asked him,
Why do you cry?
Adam said,
with his two wet eyes,
I cry because
I do not know
what day I was born.

How old am I, Eve?

And as it had done
since the very beginning
the sun came up
in the garden
the next morning.

And nothing happened
for a very long time.

And Eve
bathed in the river
that encircled
the garden.

From time to time,
while the two lovers
slept at night
under the fruit tree,
the serpent
would slip between them
to enjoy their warmth
and envy their affection
and it wished
that it had the courage
to bite them both
and make them bleed.

So Eve tickled Adam
and he laughed.

Adam fancied himself
God's favorite
in the garden.
And Eve
thought just the same
about herself.
For that matter
so did the serpent.

Can you really blame
any of them?

And Adam spent all night
counting the stars.

And a gentle breeze
passed through
the garden
disturbing the leaves
on the fruit trees
of the orchard.

Meanwhile
Eve slept among
the trees of the orchard.

Then Eve sang
the first song.

And Adam slept.

The serpent just smiled.

And the serpent
tried to sleep
but could not.

And the sun
became angry.

A _____ B _____ C _____ D _____ E _____ F _____ G _____

H _____ I _____ J _____ K _____ L _____ M _____ N _____

O _____ P _____ R _____ S _____ T _____ Z _____

z Zelda

zombie town

GAME BOARD

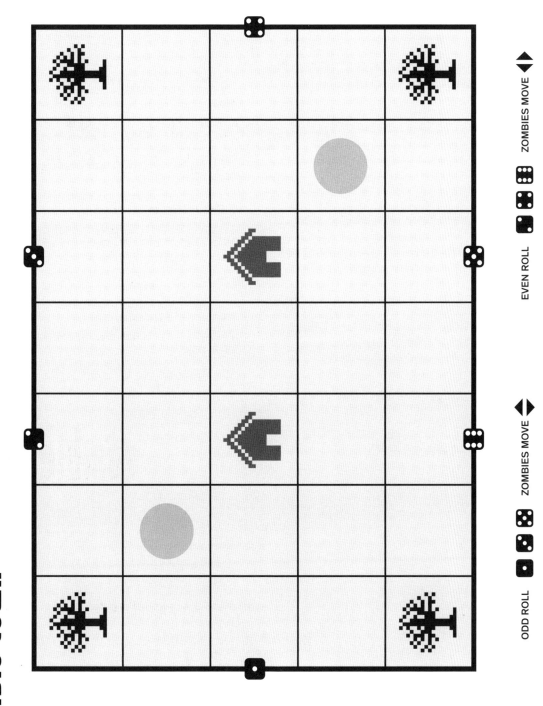

ODD ROLL ZOMBIES MOVE

EVEN ROLL ZOMBIES MOVE

zombie town

SETUP

Place your character(s) on a gray spot on the board.

Put a token marker on the 3 below to keep track of health.

PLAY

Each turn, go through the following steps in order:

1. Place a new zombie

Roll a die and place a new zombie in that space if it is empty.

(If the space is not empty, don't place a new zombie this turn.)

2. One character moves

Move any character into an adjacent empty space — or — do any special action.

A space with a tree, house, or other character is NOT empty—characters cannot move there!

3. All zombies move

Move each zombie one space toward the character that just moved or took an action:

- if the roll was even, move horizontally ◀▶
- if the roll was odd, move vertically ◆

Zombies can only move into empty spaces but will wait for each other to move out of their way if they can.

A space with a tree, house, or other character is NOT empty—zombies cannot move there!

It is possible that a Zombie will not move at all if it is already "lined up" with a character.

4. Other character moves

If there is another character, move into an adjacent empty space — or — do any special action.

5. Zombies attack!

A character loses 1 Health for each zombie in a directly adjacent space.

If a character's Health goes to zero, the character is eliminated.

If all characters die, the zombies win.

YOUR CHARACTER

Name:

What drives this character:

HEALTH (0) (1) (2) (3)

SPECIAL ACTIONS

Solo movement action:

Another solo action (something that isn't just movement):

Character combo action (involves another character):

zombie town

Name of town:

3 key facts:

A _____

B _____

C _____

D _____

E _____

F _____

G _____

H _____

I _____

J _____

K _____

L _____

M _____

N _____

O _____

P _____

R _____

S _____

T _____

Z _____

MATERIAL CONSTRAINTS

Each kind of material includes a basic suggestion for a starting point and several possible uses of that material in a game. You do not have to pick one of these uses. Feel free to mix and match, make up new mechanics, and take ideas from other materials too!

CARDS

An incredibly flexible game component. Don't get too complicated!

Start with:
Four sets of cards with numbers 1-10 on each set.

- *Use an existing deck*— Try a standard deck of cards; or the number cards from Uno; or a deck of Tarot cards
- *One or two pieces of info*— Limit each card so that it has just a few pieces of information on it, like color and number
- *Different kinds of cards*—Some cards might be special cards that break the usual format; horizontal instead of vertical?

- *Shuffle and sort*—Cards can be randomized easily, then put into stacks, hands, or spread out
- *Collect sets*—A very powerful mechanic; build melds, sort by category, or construct Poker-style hands
- *Two-sided cards*—Perhaps both sides of the cards are relevant to the gameplay
- *Cards as units*—Each card is a creature, or an emotion, or a classic work of literature

- *Cards as identity*—Each player gets a card that gives them a unique ability or assigns them to a team
- *Cards as secrets*—Nobody knows what is on your card or in your hand, but they wish they did!
- *Cards that build*—A slit cut into the cards can make them building materials; see the Eames's House of Cards

GRID

The terrain or board for your game.

Start with:
A 6×6 grid of squares with nothing special on any of the squares.

- *Classic grid*—A grid of squares. Pieces move on and occupy squares
- *Intersections*—Perhaps the pieces move on the lines and intersections, instead of or in addition to the squares
- *Missing parts*—Some of the lines or squares are missing, leading to a more mazelike space

- *Varied terrain*—There are a few different colors of spaces, each with different game effects
- *Shapes that are not squares*— The grid is made of hexagons or triangles or something else
- *A network of paths*—Rather than a grid, the game spaces are connected in more linear ways

- *Modular grid*—The board is divided into sections which can be moved or reconfigured
- *Special spaces*—There are a few key spaces that must be occupied or captured
- *Territory*—Parts of the board are owned by players, for the whole game or just at the start or end

DICE

Classic randomization device. Pro tip: avoid roll-and-move.

Start with:
One 6-sided die for each player.

- *Roll to do something*—The die number is how well you succeed at something
- *Roll and choose a die*—Roll a few dice but only choose one of them as your action
- *Sort*—After you roll them, sorting dice into groups or an order depending on what you rolled
- *Assign dice*—Roll dice, then choose how to use the number on each one in different ways

- *Match*—Try to get particular combinations of results on multiple dice
- *Poker style*—Roll a handful of dice, then choose to roll some or all of them a second time
- *Real-time rolling*—Rolling the dice as quickly as possible to try and get a particular result
- *Dice as units*—Dice can be pieces on a board or map

- *Information storage*—The number currently facing up can be used to store information
- *Design a hand of dice*—Before the game or between rounds, strategically choose which dice to roll
- *Replace the faces*—Instead of pips, change the faces into icons or other non-numerical elements
- *Hidden dice*—You keep the results of your die rolls secret

TOKENS

A subtle and versatile game component.

Start with:
50 tokens that are divided into 5 colors.

- *Instead of keeping score*— Your pile of tokens is how close you are to victory
- *Different kinds of tokens*— The size or color determines how they are used in the game
- *Collecting sets*—Try to corner the market on one color type; or collect Poker-style matches
- *Tokens as units*—Tokens are fruits, or musical notes, or unconscious desires

- *Bag them*—Put all the tokens in a cloth bag and pull out a few each turn
- *Secret tokens*—Keep your tokens hidden from other players
- *Social currency*—Your tokens are your status in the game; perhaps you can pass them when others aren't looking
- *Tokens as money*—Use them to buy things, bid for other items, or just amass your wealth

- *Blind bidding*—Each player selects tokens to bid each round without knowing other players' bids
- *Physical actions*—Depending on the tokens, they can be tossed, flicked, or stacked

TILES

Flat, stackable pieces that can be background or foreground.

Start with:
A set of Dominoes. Or a set of Scrabble tiles. Or the tiles from a Rummikub game.

- *Different shapes*—Tiles do not need to be square; they can be hexagonal, round, or irregular
- *Multiple shapes*—A variety of forms, each shape with a unique game meaning
- *Arrange into larger shapes*— As with Tangrams, build a larger object out of tiles

- *Shuffle and turn over*—Tiles can have different information on the back; you turn over one new tile each round
- *Arrange in front of you*—Keep your tiles to make sets or words or patterns
- *Stack them vertically*—Your tiles become a pile; perhaps the order of the stack is important

- *Make a board*—Each tile becomes part of a larger game board or space
- *Physical actions*—Tiles can be great as pucks or other things to shoot and flick

CARDS CARDS

GRID GRID

DICE DICE

TOKENS TOKENS

TILES TILES

Structural Constraints

The first game listed after each structure is required—you must play it. Other listed games are optional, recommended games.

Randomized Resources

Qwixx, Roll Through the Ages, Railroad Ink, Epic Spell Wars of the Battle Wizards, The Cartographers, Dice Miner

- A random mechanism gives players resources to use
- This might happen at the start of the game or every turn
- A challenge is making sure the game isn't just a random state machine but has interesting choices
- Tip: give players more than one way to make use of the resources they get

Hidden Information

Codenames, Enchanted Forest, The Resistance, Masquerade, One Night Ultimate Werewolf, Stratego

- The core of the game is that some players know things that others do not
- The information might be secret roles, or information about a map or resources
- How do you embed meaningful choices so that the game is more than just guesswork?
- Tip: as the game proceeds, make more of the hidden information visible so that the game becomes less random

Victory Points

Sushi Go, Splendor, Ticket to Ride, Tokaido, Roll Through the Ages, Settlers of Catan, Lords of Waterdeep, Kingdomino

- Players get points during the game in some way
- Whoever has the most points at the end of the game wins
- Many of these games rely on "set collection"—gathering the right elements together in order to get the most points
- Tip: give players a variety of ways to earn victory points. Can you create multiple paths to victory?

A Ticking Clock

Forbidden Island / Forbidden Desert, Pandemic, Escape: The Curse of the Temple, Heads Up, Clank, Boggle, Fortress

- Something moves the game steadily toward a conclusion
- Are there ways for players to pause or even reverse the clock?
- What happens when it reaches zero?
- Suggestion: Don't make the clock an actual real-time clock, make it tick down once per turn or round

Shared Ownership

Hanabi, Dvonn, Zertz, Colossal Arena, Cheaty Mages, El Grande, Tiny Epic Kingdoms, Acquire

- The main units or elements in the game are not owned or controlled by a specific player
- Anyone can jump in and take charge of the elements when it is their turn to play
- The key is making sure that things still can advance toward an endstate
- For example, make sure that it is not easy to simply undo what another player did

Modular Units

Cathedral, Blokus, Quantum, Galaxy Trucker, Dominion, Checkers ("kinging" a piece), Tiny Epic Quests

- Simpler parts combine into more complex wholes
- How do they fit together and what do you do with them?
- How different can you make the final combinations of parts?
- Tip: this can quickly get overcomplicated; start with a simple system and a handful of elements to combine

Repeating Short Rounds

Zombie Dice, 7 Wonders, Dixit, Resistance, Codenames, Skull

- The game plays from start to finish in a few minutes or less
- Then players get to prepare in some way before the next round starts
- Are players accumulating something between rounds?
- Are they making decisions about their setup for the next round? Or somehow improving their position?

Randomized Field of Play

Labyrinth, Forbidden Island / Forbidden Desert, Settlers of Catan, Set, Five Tribes

- When the game starts, some or all of the board, terrain, or starting conditions are randomized
- Ideally, each game feels very different; different starting combinations lead to different kinds of games
- Make sure that no one player gets a big advantage due to random luck
- Suggestion: make your game short so that you have time to playtest lots of different permutations

Real-Time Play

Magic Maze, Falling, Space Alert, Galaxy Trucker, Set, Escape: The Curse of the Temple, Pit Crew, Space Cadets Dice Duel

- Players do not take turns. They take actions (or choose to wait) whenever they want
- Build in constraints on player action, such as using only one hand, or acting once per round
- Avoid full-body sports or overly chaotic play
- The challenge here is to make a game that is real-time but still focused and strategic

Build a Network

Blokus, Waterworks Burrows, Ant Trails, Ticket to Ride, Power Grid, Tsuro, Twixt, Patchwork, Kingdomino

- Tiles or cards or board elements are used to create interlocking paths, pipes, roads, etc.
- It can be a single common network or players can each have their own network to build
- Perhaps players travel along the network, or try to build the longest or biggest network
- How do you win? By getting rid of your network elements? Or building up to a particular size?

Randomized
Resources

Hidden
Information

Victory
Points

A Ticking
Clock

Shared
Ownership

Modular
Units

Repeating
Short Rounds

Randomized
Field of Play

Real-Time
Play

Build
a Network

Afterword

I once had the pleasure of meeting Andrew Hiskens, who at the time was in charge of learning services at the State Library of Victoria in Australia. He shared with me the really interesting work he was doing at his job and particularly about one recent workshop during which they turned the tables on students and teachers. The idea of this experiment was that the students would have the opportunity to teach the teachers and not the other way around.

At the beginning of the process, he met with the children, trying to help them understand how they could teach the teachers about technology, about games, about their lives and experiences. Initially, the students had trouble wrapping their heads around this inversion of the usual classroom dynamic, but they soon took to it, giving recommendations and strategies.

As Andrew put it, one of the students told him: "OK. We understand you now. We think it could be possible to teach the teachers. But first, they really have to want to learn."

Acknowledgments

The Rules We Break is my way of saying thank you to all of the teachers and students I have encountered through the years.

First, deep gratitude to my parents, Frederick Zimmerman, Enid Zimmerman, and Gilbert Clark—who taught me (respectively) how to play, think, and design.

Grateful thanks to the teachers in my life whose lessons continue to resonate with me every day: Weezie Smith, Gary Hoff, Janice Bizzari, Pat Gleeson, Janis Stockhouse, Susan Leites, Gwynn Roberts, Elisa New, Lynda Hart, Sensei Robert Hodes, Sifu Shi Yan Ming, and Huu Rock, among so many.

Thanks to coteaching collaborators who have shown me by example how to teach from the heart: Heather Chaplin, Naomi Clark, Josh DeBonis, Clara Fernandez-Vara, Bennett Foddy, Nick Fortugno, Tracy Fullerton, Robert Hewitt, Barry Joseph, Jesper Juul, Frank Lantz, Marc LeBlanc, Richard Lemarchand, Stone Librande, Colleen Macklin, Caroline Porter, Nathalie Pozzi, Katie Salen, John Sharp, Kurt Squire, and Constance Steinkuehler.

And to all the students, staff, and faculty at the NYU Game Center, where the form and content of design education is continually debated and iterated (but we wouldn't want it any other way). That includes Matt Boch, Hermione Brice, Brendan Byrne, Logan Clare, Naomi Clark, Clara Fernandez-Vara, Bennett Foddy, Gwynna Forgham-Thrift, Jesse Fuchs, Katherine Isbister, Jesper Juul, Mitu Khandaker, Jessica Lam, Frank Lantz, Jason Leahey, Rosanne Limoncelli, mattie, Dylan McKenzie, Matt Parker, Shawn Pierre, Toni Pizza, Charles Pratt, Winnie Song, Kevin Spain, Ayanna Wilson, and Robert Yang.

A host of design educators playtested these exercises and gave crucial feedback, even from the depths of a global pandemic. Thanks for playing: Daniel Ames, Elizabeth Ballou, Thom Bartscherer, Matt Callahan, Irwin Chen, Adam Clare, Doug Clark, Ramiro Corbetta, Melanie Crean, Josh Debonis, Cynthia Dias, Blake Eskin, Federico Fasce, Alex Fleetwood, Aaron Freedman, Tracy Fulleron, Jessica Hammer, Greg Heffernan, Nicolas Hesler, Robert Hewitt, Jesper Juul, Jonaya Kemper, Cody Kiker, Alexander King, Lynn Kirabo, Josh Laison, Richard Lemarchand, Stone Librande, Jay Little, JingJin Liu, Colleen Macklin, Nik Mikros, Sevan Mujukian, Kevin O'Connor, Scot Osterwile, Jason Oualline, Jeff Pidsadny, Karina Popp, Katie Salen, Ian Schreiber, John Sharp, Kurt Squire, Constance Steinkhuler, Jimi Stine, Ben Stokes, Tess Tanenbaum, Aaron Trammel, Chris Wallace, Jason Weiser, and Keenan Yoho.

This book was a collaboration from start to finish, and could never have happened without the profoundly insightful input of editor Jennifer Thompson, the deliciously sharp visual design of Ben English, and help from Sara Stemen and the rest of the fantastic team at Princeton Architectural Press. Thanks to publisher Lynn Grady for taking on this unusual project and to Kevin O'Connor for generously introducing me in the first place.

Heartfelt thanks for painfully spicy and critically close readings of the manuscript by Solon Simmons, Aaron Stalnaker, Kirsten Sword, Keenan Yoho, and Enid Zimmerman.

And finally, thanks to ruthless feedback from Nathalie Pozzi, whose beautiful mind and exacting sensibility has had an indelible impact on just about every page of this book. And on the rest of my life too.

Easy is shit.

Leonard Zimmerman

Published by
Princeton Architectural Press
70 West 36th Street
New York, NY 10018
www.papress.com

Editor: Jennifer Thompson
Designer: Benjamin English

Library of Congress Cataloging-in-Publication Data
Names: Zimmerman, Eric, 1969– author.
Title: The rules we break : lessons in play, thinking, and
    design / Eric Zimmerman.
Description: First edtion. | New York : Princeton Architectural
    Press, [2022] | Includes bibliographical references. |
    Summary: "Games and exercises to help designers
    understand how people think, how systems work, and how
    a design process can unfold" —Provided by publisher.
Identifiers: LCCN 2022019115 (print) | LCCN 2022019116
    (ebook) | ISBN 9781648960673 (paperback) | ISBN
    9781648962066 (ebook)
Subjects: LCSH: System design--Technique. | Engineering
    design—Technique. | Gamification. | Play. | Thought
    experiments. | Critical thinking.
Classification: LCC TA174 .Z56 2022 (print) | LCC TA174
    (ebook) | DDC 620/.004—dc23/eng/20220505
LC record available at https://lccn.loc.gov/2022019115
LC ebook record available at https://lccn.loc.
    gov/2022019116

Credits
page 18: Bernard De Koven with Holly Gramazio, edited by
Celia Pearce and Eric Zimmerman, *The Infinite Playground*,
excerpt for epigraph use, © 2020 Massachusetts Institute
of Technology, by permission of The MIT Press.
page 66: Reprinted from *Thinking in Systems*, copyright
©2008 used with permission from Chelsea Green Publishing
Co., White River Junction, Vermont (www.chelseagreen.com).